CW01653111

£10

Building Classic Salmon Flies

Building Classic Salmon Flies

RON ALCOTT

Foreword by DICK STEWART

Edited by ARLEIGH D. RICHARDSON III

Photographs by the Author

The Countryman Press

WOODSTOCK, VERMONT

The Countryman Press, Inc.
PO Box 175, Woodstock, Vermont 05091-0175
Published simultaneously in Canada by Nimbus Publishing Limited

Text and photographs © 1995 by Ronald K. Alcott
Foreword © 1995 by Richard B. Stewart

All rights reserved. No part of this book may be reproduced in any form or by any electronic or mechanical means including information storage and retrieval systems without permission in writing from the publisher, except by a reviewer, who may quote brief passages.

Some of the material in this book has appeared in different form in *American Angler & Fly Tyer, American Angler,* and the *Atlantic Salmon Journal.*

Library of Congress Cataloging-in-Publication Data
Alcott, Ron, 1934–
Building classic salmon flies / Ron Alcott ; foreword by Dick Stewart ; edited by Arleigh D. Richardson III ; photographs by the author.
p. cm.
Includes bibliographical references (p. 189) and index.
ISBN 0-88150-314-2
1. Fly tying. 2. Flies, Artificial. 3. Atlantic salmon fishing. I. Richardson, Arleigh D. (Arleigh Dygert) II. Title.
SH451.A44 1995
688.7'912—dc20
95-18384
CIP

Printed in Canada
10 9 8 7 6 5 4 3 2 1

Cover photograph by Ron Alcott © 1995
Book design by Susan Hood
Artwork by Paul Anthony and Rhonda Alcott-Hyson © 1995

CONTENTS

Dedication

For my wife, Lillian, and our sons and daughters,
Mark, Brian, Rhonda, and Brenda

Foreword

More experienced editors might have thought me crazy, but being a neophyte to the editor's desk some years back, I didn't know that most magazines refuse handwritten manuscripts. My only concern was that Ron Alcott was willing to share his knowledge, ideas, and skills, and I felt my job was to transcribe his longhand for the benefit of our readers. So I agreed to publish his article on classic featherwing Atlantic salmon flies in *American Angler & Fly Tyer* magazine.

I was planning to photograph two of Ron Alcott's handsome Jock Scotts for the magazine's front cover. However, Ron trusted neither the mail nor the photographer; so he drove three hours on a Sunday morning to hand-deliver the flies. He remained through the photo session to ensure that every fiber was in proper position when the shutter was tripped. Prior to that day, we knew each other only through mutual friends, reputation, and some telephone conversations, but this first collaboration resulted in my later working with Ron on a number of articles about the art of dressing traditional Atlantic salmon flies. Thus began a rapport that continues to this day, a friendship established on respect, both professional and personal.

Readers of this book need to know that its author is no newcomer to his craft: Ron Alcott has certainly paid his dues. Disenchanted as a commercial tyer of trout flies, Ron decided to pursue the tying of Atlantic salmon flies. In fact, he took a year off from work to devote himself exclusively to learning all he could, from whomever he could. Possibly it was his lack of formal education that drove him toward achievement, perhaps other forces—I don't know. Regardless of the motivation, I'm constantly amazed at his accumulation of information and his ability to quote chapter and verse from either Kelson, Hale, or Pryce-Tannatt as he struggles to give order and reason to some of the obscure documentation of his chosen vocation. I'm equally awed at the in-depth ornithological research he's conducted in order to be fully informed regarding the various plumages utilized in the construction of the flies. And I know of his repute among fly-shop personnel for his rummaging searches through their bins of fly-tying materials, examining feathers until he finds "just the right ones."

If practice makes perfect, then Ron certainly qualifies as a teacher of fly-tying, for his calling has taken him throughout much of the United States and Canada. I could also comment on Ron's meticulous attention to the smallest detail in his flies, or his consummate concern for their proper presentation, but I think these aspects are adequately confirmed by his contributions to Joe Bates's *The Art of the Atlantic Salmon Fly*, Judith Dunham's *The Atlantic Salmon Fly, Flies for Atlantic Salmon* by Farrow Allen and myself, as well as the *Atlantic Salmon Journal.*

This book is a sharing. In these pages Ron Alcott's greatest hope is that he might be able to present the first unique instructional guide since Pryce-Tannatt's *How to Dress Salmon Flies*—one that will help tyers demystify an arcane craft and transform it into an enjoyable art form. My greatest admiration, however, is reserved for Ron's willingness to share everything he has learned with anyone who is interested. There are no secrets here, no holding back—for above all, Ron is a teacher.

DICK STEWART
NORTH CONWAY, NEW HAMPSHIRE

Acknowledgments

My goal has never been to find fame in building flies. My motivation is to be remembered. To achieve that, it is necessary to have a broad knowledge of a subject and be willing to share that study and experience with others. To be remembered for learning and giving something important to others far outweighs the insignificant gain anyone ever receives from opportunism. Teaching is important because of its noteworthy results and the influence it has on the accumulated knowledge of any particular field. I am humbled and flattered to receive the ultimate compliment of being imitated by so many of you who have asked me to make a record of the many hours of enjoyment we have shared together in classes, demonstrations, and conversations.

A problem that I can't solve is how to name here all of you who have supported me, since it isn't practical to have a whole chapter of names. Therefore, I have to ask you to accept my expression of regret for not being able to do it. Never forget that I hold each of you in high esteem and remember your encouragement.

Yet, there are among my very good friends some who have had a very direct influence on my achievements. They are not listed in any order, but as a group who gave special support to the cause. They are Megan Boyd, B.E.M., Bill Blackstone, Al Cohen, Dave and Bert Fram, Jim and Karen Murray, Dick Stewart, Bob Warren, Rob Solo, Jerry King, Ed Story, Eleanor H. Stickney, photography consultant Diane Van

Dusen, my uncle Art Childs, the past and present staff of the Atlantic Salmon Federation, the late Colonel Joseph D. Bates, and the late Fran Stuart. Prominent among this group for his hard work typing, revising, and correcting this book is Dick Richardson. Dick is to the English language what feathers are to salmon flies.

I owe all of you a large debt of gratitude.

Introduction

The purpose of this book is twofold. The first is to demonstrate, through pictures and text, how to build featherwing salmon flies of the types shown in the color plates. The second is to answer the questions most often asked by students during my ten years of giving classes in building flies of this kind.

Perhaps the students' most common question is how to interpret what was written in the nineteenth and early twentieth centuries and how to translate the terms and practices of those times into practical and effective guidance for today's fly-tyer. For answers I have had to draw on historical material from works that are not readily available today. I have attempted here to be an intermediary between those early writers and the reader, and have cited the works as necessary. As my intent is to answer as many of those questions as possible, I ask my readers to remember that what may not be of particular interest to one may mean a great deal to someone else.

Beginning, intermediate, and advanced fly-tyers can use this book. I would strongly encourage beginners, however, to get some preliminary practice in building simpler flies, such as streamers or trout wet flies, since this is not intended as a beginner's manual of basic fly-tying. Admittedly, building featherwing salmon flies, with their forty or more different steps, can seem like an obstacle course to the completely inexperienced. On the other hand, with some basic practice and a modicum of self-confidence, any tyer should be able to follow the steps given in the text and photos. Each of us has to start somewhere, and the world still awaits that perfectly built fly.

I should also say that although featherwing salmon flies are in some ways a breed unto themselves, building them involves certain techniques that can profitably be applied to the building of hairwing salmon flies, trout flies, and others. Doubling hackles, making ropes of dubbing, tying in tinsel, setting vertical wings, and marrying wing strips are just a few that come to mind. I have used these techniques on my own trout and hairwing salmon flies, with the resulting benefit of enhanced quality and durability. It also follows that featherwings can be used for fishing! In their earliest days, of course, that was their only purpose. Of late, they have been regarded primarily as creations for exhibition and collecting, but they are still being fished for salmon. This was corroborated recently when a good friend in Corner Brook, Newfoundland, invited me to fish the Humber River in the 1995 season. While we discussed what flies to bring, his statement "They'll take a classic, size 2/0" brought a smile to my face. There is surely no reason not to build classic flies for fishing. Not everyone is a collector, and to be fished, flies don't have to be of exhibition quality. The basic requirement is to use conventional wire-eye hooks and reduce their size from 4/0. Tying and successfully fishing a classic featherwing fly can greatly enhance the charm and pleasure of fishing for Atlantic salmon.

As this book is meant to be *used,* the following brief chapter summaries may be helpful to the reader.

Chapter one contains a short account of the history of salmon flies, which I hope will add to the tyer's enjoyment of the art and hobby.

Chapter two identifies by name and country of origin the rare exotic types of feathers originally used in building featherwing salmon flies, as well as more practical and perfectly acceptable alternatives for today's use. Feathers that continue to be readily available in shops that specialize in salmon fly-tying materials are also listed. There is also some discussion of non-avian components of featherwings such as seal's fur, pig's wool, Berlin wool, and silk.

Chapter three examines colors for feathers, furs, and silks, explaining historical colors and the confusion caused by earlier nomenclature. Colors for contemporary tyers are identified by name and displayed in a color chart.

Chapter four covers metallic tinsels and explains some of the different names used for these materials.

Chapter five deals with what many consider the most confusing subject in this field: the different types of wings used in classic salmon flies. These wings and their manner of construction are covered in detail.

Chapter six is devoted to proportion, an extremely important aspect of any fly. The chapter instructs how to establish proportions and how to incorporate them into featherwing salmon flies.

Chapter seven solves the mystery of how to build a classic fly through a series of pictures, explanations, and interpretations.

Chapter eight lists twenty-five fly patterns. For the sake of custom, the rare feathers are named in the dressings. The reader can consult chapter two for recommended alternatives for today's use.

To my knowledge, this is the first book in recent years devoted solely to a comprehensive study of building featherwing salmon flies. My suggestion for further exploration of the subject is Pryce-Tannatt's *How to Tie Salmon Flies* (see bibliography).

Finally, you might ask why I chose the term *building* for the title. With hundreds of hours at the vise, and with nearly as much time to think about what I was doing, I've concluded that I *build* a fly. The steps involved in preparing materials, from measurement with a ruler, through locating exactly where they fit, to ending by painting on a finish coat for the head, all lead to the conclusion that a fly is built by stages. Compare it with building a wall for a house. If a stud is too long, too short, or, even worse, warped, it cannot be used. The solution is to select another that is of the correct length and straight. After that, the builder has to measure for sixteen inches on center. It is exactly the same process with feathers. Each has to be measured, or at least judged well, for correct size. Nevertheless, a fly is not finished unless it is tied together. Therefore, I look at tying as a process in building a fly, as hammering nails is a part of building a wall. So when I build a fly, I concentrate on how I want the fly to look when it's finished, and build it accordingly.

Some of the patterns in this book are more complex than others, but none is beyond the capabilities of anyone who wants to become proficient at building featherwing flies. No matter how dressing/building techniques are learned, whether by self teaching, in classes, or from written instructions, no notable degree of success will be accomplished without practice. Techniques have to be repeated until they become habitual. In the past decade a lot of beautifully dressed flies have been showing up. The best are by dressers who have accepted the fact that they must practice. A number of things contribute to dressing nice flies, such as good materials, determination, and wanting to succeed, but none of it will come together without a hell of a lot of practice.

In short, with this book, the road to success is to read the text carefully, study the illustrations, and again *practice.* The only person you have to satisfy is yourself.

Chapter One

Lessons from the Past

Salmon flies developed from trout flies, and both were originally of a commonplace character and dull in appearance. The leap forward to bright featherwing salmon flies with exotic feathers appears to have gained strength and reached its greatest extent in the latter part of the nineteenth century. The popularity of these flies for fishing prevailed into the twentieth century.

In the 1930s and 1940s, hairwing flies began to take over. I believe that the unavailability of many exotic materials, coupled with very high prices for those rare feathers that were available, played a major role in the decline of traditional featherwing salmon flies.

Since the 1950s, hairwings have been the predominant flies for Atlantic salmon fishing. This is not to say that the beautiful featherwings died a sudden death. Many popular patterns are still being fished. Even though hair replaced feathers in the wings, a fascination with the "classics" has revived interest in featherwings, and they are now considered a challenge to build and are thought of as works of art. Most are now framed and displayed in collections.

My first book on dressing salmon flies was Eric Taverner's *Salmon Fishing,* published in 1935. In it, he identifies many of the established feathers that I had previously known only by name. He recommends alternative feathers to replace some of the exotics, and his comment that cock-of-the-rock would hardly be missed because of its poor quality can be interpreted as his indifference to the unavailability of certain specific feathers. His comment was inspiring, for I thought contemporary fly-dressers were adhering too rigidly to the use of mandated feathers in building featherwing salmon flies. At the time, the accepted view was that without them, flies would be inferior and inadequate.

Thereafter, as I added books to my collection, more references surfaced advocating various feathers as replacements for the scarce or unavailable exotics. Each author justifies the use of interchangeable materials simply because of the unavailability of a particular kind of feather.

Two early books—George Cole Bainbridge's *The Fly Fisher's Guide* and P. Fisher's *The Angler's Souvenir* (published in 1816 and 1835, respectively)—are a joy to read. Although lacking in descriptions and applications of customary feathers, each offers interesting historical insights. Bainbridge writes about such things as grass and horse-hair fly lines, which gender of horse has the best quality of hair for fly lines, and the belief that a cock salmon uses its kype to help the hen salmon prepare a redd. Of interest to all fly-dressers is that the book was the first to have a hand-colored plate of salmon flies.

Fisher's book covers all types of fishing, and is also a pleasure to read. The woodcut illustrations and page borders are beautiful. However, it is elementary with regard to building salmon flies. Nevertheless, it does give excellent examples of early fly-dressers' use of unusual materials. For example, Fisher tells of a friend's visit to a zoological garden that results in one of the friend's flies having "the wings formed of the feathers of a condor, variegated with the plumage of a macaw. The body is formed of the undergrowth of a lion's mane, and the whiskers are from the beard of a leopard." (I don't doubt for a moment the use of strange materials, but I would like to know how they got the leopard's whiskers.)

The second edition of J.H. Hale's *How to Tie Salmon Flies* (published in 1919) contains an appendix of 344 dressings and also lists feathers that were not used in standard dressings. These include bittern hackles, cockatoo tails, cuckoo dun hackles, snipe feathers, shovel duck, mandarin drake, and Egyptian goose.

In the fifth edition of *A Book on Angling* (published in 1880), Francis Francis also mentions a few obscure feathers, such as purple lory and flamingo. His recipe for the Dhom gives the option of using kingfisher or chatterer for the fly's cheeks. All of Francis Francis's dressings refer to *ribs,* which are what we today call *horns.*

After a variety of alternative types of feathers, the next things that became apparent were changes of components in separate dressings for a fly with the same name. For example, in the Dusty Miller Francis Francis has a wing composed of golden pheasant tail, mallard, teal, green parrot, and lavender swan. However, Hale's second edition lists that pattern's wing as having black turkey with white tips, golden pheasant tail, bustard, pintail, guinea fowl, and mallard. And T.E. Pryce-Tannatt's *How to Dress Salmon Flies* prescribes a white-tipped turkey underwing with married strands of teal; yellow, scarlet, and orange swan; bustard; florican; and golden pheasant tail.

Looking for standardization in featherwings is labor in vain. All flytyers have their own unique styles of building flies. That alone will prevent the establishment of any criteria, because no two tyers can dress identical flies. One tyer can influence another to the extent that there will be close similarities in the way a particular fly is built, but no one has been able to prescribe how a fly should be dressed in such a way as to set an absolute standard. It will never happen because no one has ever dressed, nor will anyone ever dress, a perfect fly. The perfect fly is, in any event, a physical impossibility, because no two feathers are exactly the same. Therefore, why have secrets in dressing methods? I believe that secrets hinder advancement and success in the art. Without fresh ideas, progress will be limited.

Prerequisite to building these flies is understanding the meaning of "classic salmon flies." The best explanation I've found is on page two of Pryce-Tannatt's first edition:

> There is an indescribable something about a fly dressed by an expert amateur, who is a practical salmon fisherman, which the fly dressed by a non-angling professional not infrequently lacks. I have heard this peculiar quality rather neatly referred to as 'soul.' A precise explanation of what is meant by 'soul' is one of the impossibilities. The term is incomprehensible to the uninitiated, but is completely understood by the experienced man.

Chapter Two

Materials and Substitutes

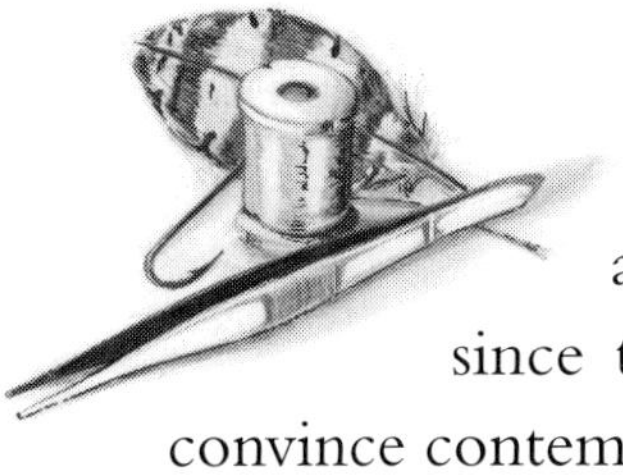

This chapter addresses the widespread use of alternative materials that has been going on since the early eighteenth century. My intent is to convince contemporary tyers to "make peace with the past" and realize that beautiful flies can be built using alternative feathers, and that in some patterns, alternative feathers indeed make a much better looking fly. Also, the present-day unavailability of some exotic feathers, import restrictions, and exorbitant prices for what is available are themselves justification for the use of alternatives. I consider "substitute materials" a poor choice of words and use the term "alternative materials" in this book.

For examples of the types of feathers listed in this chapter, please refer to color plates 1 and 2.

Indian Crow

This is the red-ruffed fruit crow. Its five subspecies are indigenous to South America. White feathers from the neck of a Chinese ringneck pheasant or from the neck of a hen chicken, dyed red, provide an adequate alternative. Small, shell-shaped golden pheasant crest feathers (found at the base of the crest where they meet the tippets) colored with permanent inks work especially well to duplicate the texture and appearance of Indian crow.

Bustards

Not to argue with tradition, but I believe the term *speckled,* as it is traditionally applied to this bird, is something of a misnomer. A bustard feather has fine-textured barring, varying in length perpendicular to the quill. As the barring extends toward either edge of the feather, the length of the bars decreases until they appear as speckles or spots. It is used primarily in wing strips and occasionally for throats and tail veilings.

Another type of bustard commonly used is florican. In fly-dressings, the florican used comes from the great bustard *(Otis tarda).* Pryce-Tannatt refers to the "boldly barred black and cinnamon ones from the European species." This is because the great bustard was, in earlier times, indigenous to Europe. Two species of true florican are found in India and China. Had Pryce-Tannatt mentioned the great bustard as the one used, less confusion would have resulted.

There are many variations of mottled turkeys that are excellent alternatives to both light- and dark-speckled bustard. The black-and-tan side tail feathers next to the two center tail feathers of Lady Amherst pheasant serve very well in place of florican. The center tails, dyed tan, can also be used.

Blue Chatterer

Why is the blue chatterer usually singled out as the only feather used as cheeks and tail veilings on salmon flies? Chatterer has always been extremely rare. This is made clear both in books displaying pictures of antique flies and in flies themselves. There is a noticeable lack of blue chatterer in most of them. Because of its rarity and the fact that kingfisher appears in much earlier works than those by Hale, Kelson, and Pryce-Tannatt, finding chatterer should not be a priority. Alternatives for blue chatterer are listed under kingfisher.

Kingfisher

A reliable way to distinguish kingfisher from chatterer is to check the color at the base of the feathers; kingfisher is gray while chatterer is black. Kingfisher should not be considered inferior to chatterer. Alternatives for both, if kingfisher isn't available, are small hen chicken neck feathers dyed kingfisher blue.

Jay

The first thing to keep in mind is that the North American blue jay is a protected songbird. It is important to point that out, because a contemporary book published in England names the North American jay as the type used in featherwing salmon flies. (That book also contains inaccuracies regarding other feathers.) The type of jay used by fly-dressers is the European jay. The only feathers used from this bird are the blue-gray-black lesser covert (shoulder) wing feathers. The barred side of the feather is quite short in barb length and can be used only on smaller-sized salmon flies. Pryce-Tannatt recommended guinea fowl dyed blue as the alternative.

Cock-of-the-Rock

This bird is indigenous to northern South America. Taverner says very succinctly, "The breast and the back feathers of the Cock-of-the-rock were very little used, and therefore will be hardly missed." He was writing about the restrictions on the importation of certain foreign birds into England. The feathers are flimsy and difficult to work with. Hen chicken feathers, dyed to match the real thing, can actually produce a much better looking fly.

Jungle Cock

The earliest written reference to jungle cock being used in salmon flies was around 1850. Although off the market for some time, in the past couple of years jungle cock feathers have again become available through some retailers. Remember, too, there are some beautiful patterns that do not call for them.

Heron

It's doubtful that any North American heron played a role in dressing the Scottish Dee and other patterns calling for heron. Surely it was the European and African species, which were much more accessible to European tyers. Heron is used as body hackles and throats. Alternatives include ringneck pheasant rump feathers dyed black or gray; the best, however, are blue-, brown-, or white-eared pheasants dyed the appropriate color. Heron is a protected species, and it is illegal to sell the feathers.

Scarlet Ibis

This bird is indigenous to Central America and northern South America. Its red color is due to its feeding primarily on shrimp. As with heron, scarlet ibis is protected. It is strictly prohibited to sell feathers from either species. The best approach is to look for an alternative feather.

The natural color of ibis leaves a lot to be desired when compared to a brilliant dyed red goose feather, and the latter makes a much more attractive fly. When only narrow strips in a tail or wing veiling are needed, red macaw or red undertail feathers from African gray parrots are also good alternatives.

Toucan

Historically, toucan feathers were used as tails, tail veilings, jointed-body veilings, and occasionally as a throat. Small, shell-shaped golden pheasant crest feathers (found on the crest where they meet the tippets) are great as an alternative. This is the same feather identified as an alternative for Indian crow.

Macaw

Three types of macaw feathers from the tail are used at various times. They are scarlet, blue-and-yellow (same feather), and blue-and-scarlet (same feather).

Eagle

Eagle feathers are most important, from a legal point of view. Specifically, they cannot be possessed in the United States without a federal permit. For the Yellow and Gray-Eagle Dee patterns, pheasant rump feathers dyed yellow or gray are good alternatives.

Waterfowl

Waterfowl feathers are readily available through materials shops, with the exception of European widgeon. When patterns calling for widgeon were originated, they obviously used the European widgeon.

North American widgeon is brown in color on its flanks. European widgeon is similar to pintail or mallard flank with its grayish-black striped feathers. Used as a throat, one would be hard to distinguish from the other. Most teal flank feathers sold in shops for wing strips and veilings are actually pintail, because teal is not long enough to make wing strips.

Wood duck, with its black-and-white barred flank feathers, was a threatened species during the early part of the twentieth century. Since the 1950s, however, the species has made a strong recovery, and its feathers are inventoried in some materials shops. Early writers sometimes referred to wood duck as *summer duck*.

Bronze mallard is used as a *roofing* for some classic flies that call for it, and it is also available in shops that carry salmon fly materials.

Other Common Feathers

The following feathers are plentiful and therefore readily available.

Chinese Necks

Chinese necks come from the necks of roosters. I use them exclusively for body hackle. In addition to colors listed under schlappen or listed in the dressings in chapter eight, Chinese necks in badger dyed yellow and golden olive are also required.

Saddle Hackles

Saddle hackles come from the backs of roosters. I use them occasionally for throat hackles, but never for body hackles.

Schlappen

Schlappen comes from the tails of roosters. It is ninety-five percent webbed and makes excellent throats. Its basic colors are red, fiery brown, orange, bright orange, green, light blue, blue, dark blue, magenta, claret, scarlet, crimson, black, and yellow.

Plate 1 FEATHERS

1. Scarlet Ibis
2. Toucan
3. Vulturine Guinea Fowl
4. Golden Olive Hackle
5. White-Tipped Turkey
6. Blue Chatterer
7. Indian Crow
8. Peacock Wing
9. Cinnamon Turkey
10. Kenya Crested Guinea Fowl
11. Lady Amherst Pheasant Tippet
12. Scarlet Macaw
13. Golden Pheasant Crest Colored as Indian Crow
14. Blue-and-Yellow Macaw
15. Golden Pheasant Sword
16. Golden Pheasant Tippet
17. Mottled Turkey
18. Cock-of-the-Rock
19. Mottled Turkey (alternate for speckled bustard)
20. European Jay
21. Jungle Cock
22. Kingfisher
23. Golden Pheasant Tail

Plate 2 FEATHERS *(continued)*

24. Black-and-White Barred Wood Duck
25. Pintail
26. Dark Speckled Bustard
27. Light Speckled Bustard
28. Bronze Mallard
29. Florican Bustard

Golden Pheasant

Crest, neck tippets, and tail are the most widely used pheasant feathers, although some patterns call for an underwing of red body feathers as well as red sword feathers.

Lady Amherst Pheasant

Lady Amherst tippets are the primary wing feather in the Lady Amherst, Colonel's Lady, and Lady Lillian patterns. The two center tail feathers of the Lady Amherst pheasant are used as parts of wings in a number of other flies.

Ostrich

Dyed black, ostrich is the mainstay for butts. A few exhibition patterns require ostrich in red, white, and blue.

Turkey

Turkey tail feathers are found in speckled, brown, dark brown, white-tipped, cinnamon, mottled, and natural black.

Guinea Fowl

Guinea fowl hackles, both natural and dyed blue, are used in many patterns—particularly the back feathers, which are speckled.

Peacock

Secondary peacock wing feathers, swords, and herl are often called for.

Goose

In lieu of swan, goose feathers in yellow, blue, red, orange, green, black, white, and sometimes claret are the basics for wing strips. Swans have had Crown protection in England in the past, and their feathers are still sometimes difficult to get. The second and third editions of Hale's *How to Tie Salmon Flies* have this to say: "Swan . . . when dyed are very useful for wings. Feathers from the common white goose . . . dye equally well, and are very largely used." The significance of this statement is that it shows that alternative materials have been widely used since early times.

The materials mentioned so far in this chapter are the main ingredients for the majority of salmon flies. They were identified in Hardy Brothers' second edition of Hale's book.

A few of the more obscure materials listed in patterns are: ringneck cock and hen pheasant tails, shovel duck, cuckoo hackles, snipe, black cockatoo tail, Egyptian goose, donkey fur, hare's ear fur, horse hair, silver monkey hair, American squirrel fur, and goldbeater's skin (which is prepared from the large intestine of an ox). The only need to have these and other relatively unknown materials is when a rare pattern specifically calls for them.

Furs, Wools, and Silks

Seal

Required seal's fur colors are the same as those listed above under schlappen, with the exception of magenta. If seal's fur is not available, African goat is an excellent alternative, and it is easier to work because of its finer staple.

Pig's Wool

Pig's wool comes from the ears and under the chins of pigs. The guard hairs were picked out and the remaining hair was used in bodies of flies. Pig's wool appears to have fallen out of favor early in the evolution of salmon flies because of its texture, which can be likened to extra-fine steel wool.

Mohair

Mohair is used as a body veiling and occasionally as a collar.

Silk

It is important to find a quality of silk that is easy to work with. Two criteria must be met: The silk should be easy to split into finer plies so that bulky tags can be avoided, and it should wind flat around the hook. Silks that meet these criteria are available in tackle and yarn shops that inventory silks.

Wool

The predominant color requirements for wool are red and black, for butts and heads. A type of wool often referred to in early books is Berlin wool. This wool comes from merino sheep, a fine-wool breed that originated in Spain and became popular in America, Australia, and Germany. The breed excels in its quality of fleece, and its wool was widely used in embroidery cross-stitch. The German wool was sent to Berlin for dyeing, hence the name. Unfortunately, true Berlin wool is no longer available, but its staple can be duplicated. Take ordinary wool, as fine in fiber as possible, pull it apart, and break the fibers into very short lengths. A recommended method to break it up (though one I have never tried) is to cut it into quarter-inch sections and run it through a blender.

CHAPTER THREE

Silk, Feather, and Fur Colors

One of the most difficult things in tying flies from description is to hit off the right shade of colour. I have done my best to overcome this difficulty in point of description, but, more or less it must always exist, and the fly tyer must not be angry with me if I find myself unable, out of twenty shades of green, for example, to describe in words any particular shade beyond the possibility.

FRANCIS FRANCIS,
A BOOK ON ANGLING

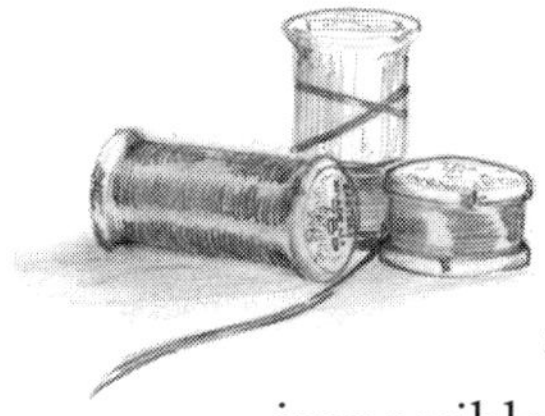

Volumes have been written trying to sort out the intricate tangle in the realm of color. Colors have an enigmatic character that makes precise description impossible. When a person tries to describe in words a color seen in his mind's eye, it is all but impossible to do so without reference to another color similar to the one in question. The same can be said about reading a description of a color. The words are real, but they are not accurately understood. Description is not possible without a clear reference that defines the precise color meant. For our purpose, the only satisfactory method of defining the color of a silk is to have either samples of the original silk or specimens of the flies themselves.

Assuming it were possible to meet these conditions, the description still might not be completely accurate. Silks, as well as other materials, are not dyed now to duplicate colors that were available during the height of the classic salmon fly period.

Historic Colors and Terminology

Comparing the pigment colors available today with those used in the early nineteenth century will show the differences between them.

Until the mid-1850s, various species of plants and trees were used to produce organic dyes. The second half of that century brought the introduction of aniline dyes, whose terminology is not always clear in the early books on tying salmon flies.

Of the many unfamiliar terms, those most often asked about are probably *lake* and *madder. Lake* refers to a process of pigment manufacture in which organic coloring matter is used with a base or carrier of inorganic material. The word is also applied to a group of reddish colors, such as crimson lake, scarlet lake, purple lake, and madder lake, to name only a few; and there are still more colors associated with lake that depended on the types of materials used to make them. But all of them had lake pigment as an ingredient.

Madder has two meanings. It refers to any of the plants of the genus *Rubia,* and especially a Eurasian species, *R. tinctorum.* Prior to the twentieth century, the root was an important source for dyes, and the pigment quality was noted for its permanence. As with *lake,* the term *madder* also denotes a family of related colors. Brown madder, for example, is a lake pigment prepared from madder root, and is a deep, rich brown. Colors with madder as an ingredient ranged from brown to yellow, and rose through red to deep purple. We can see from Hale's *How to Tie Salmon Flies* that his method of dyeing fiery brown was to use either Brazilwood, logwood (the heartwood of a Central American tree in the senna family), or madder. Hale's listing of three possible materials makes it clear there was no standard to follow when dyeing fly-tying materials.

Many tyers (and I include myself), when reading Francis Francis, are mystified trying to determine the color referred to as *light purple* in the dressing for #4 on page 402[1], and the footnote only adds to the mystery. It reads, "This is a difficult color to describe, as it is neither claret, nor red, nor purple, nor puce, nor mulberry, nor mauve; it is more the old-fashioned color called 'lake'." In his mind's eye, Francis Francis knew the color, but today it's anyone's guess.

As early as the 1890s there was concern about this lack of standardization for the colors of silks, furs, and feathers used by fly-tyers. Hale even devoted a page to saying that dyeing materials had not received attention toward improvement equal to what other branches of the sport had. His comment reads in part: "The colors offered for sale at the present time are, in most cases, no better than they were thirty years ago, notwithstanding the fact that hundreds of dyes producing different shades of color have been discovered." Hale adds, ". . . some of the old-fashioned wood dyes give us colors . . . which cannot be beaten by aniline dyes." He cites the example of the aforementioned fiery brown.

There is the story of Michael Rogan, a famous Irish tyer of the period, who reportedly used donkey urine in the dyeing of fiery brown, a color for which Rogan was renowned. One version of the story is that there were vats of donkey urine stacked through his yard, smelling up the neighborhood. Mr. Rogan may well have had nothing more than a unique home-brewed method of dyeing fiery brown. The urine was used not as a dye but as a fixative, to help set the pigment. This method is also mentioned in William Blacker's *Blacker's Art of Fly Making* (published in 1855), where in his instructions on how to dye orange, he writes, ". . . and afterwards rinse them in urine which gives luster and softness to the stuff." The question is, then, why donkey

1. A large number of flies in this book are not named, but are listed by number from different regions in Great Britain.

urine? Surely a busy fly-tyer would not have had the time to stand around with a long stick to which a cup was attached waiting for the right moment. In actuality, a pH of four would have worked, and each chamber pot would have contained some!

Natural dyes—animal, vegetable, and mineral—were important to early tyers, not so much because of their undoubted quality, but because there was nothing else available. With the introduction of chemical dyes, most requirements for specific colors were easily met. The nineteenth-century manufacturing process used to make a single shade of a specific color often resulted in the manufacturer assigning his special name to it. This resulted in many instances when the same shade had several names, depending on the number of manufacturers producing it. Also, a single dye often took differently on different materials. This accounts for the mystery surrounding some of the early color names, such as Bismarck brown, referred to in Kelson's *The Salmon Fly*. *Webster's Third International Dictionary* describes Bismarck brown as a "yellowish brown," used in dyeing cotton, jute, wool, leather, and silk. One reason for the obscurity of the color is its having been listed in a nineteenth-century dictionary not among the standard color chips, but on a separate chart listing dye colors. To further confuse the issue, that same chart of dye colors contains two distinctly different shades of brown, each labeled Bismarck brown!

Furthermore, the use of nouns and adjectives to designate colors made it difficult to establish a standard within the trade. Any manufacturing process that makes colors cannot provide only names for those colors. Words simply are not sufficiently precise to describe accurately a particular shade. Consequently, numbers were introduced to designate colors and shades of color, and are used to this day in the color and dye industries. Numbers do not solve the problem completely, however. In his widely used book, Pryce-Tannatt writes that of the hundreds of different available shades, and after looking in his fly box, he finds ". . . for the past four years, and for all many *[sic]* of flies: 7A, 156A, 160 . . ." There is no hint of what these colors were.

There are further ambiguities in Pryce-Tannatt's color terminology. In his instructions for the Jock Scott, the rear half of the body is to be

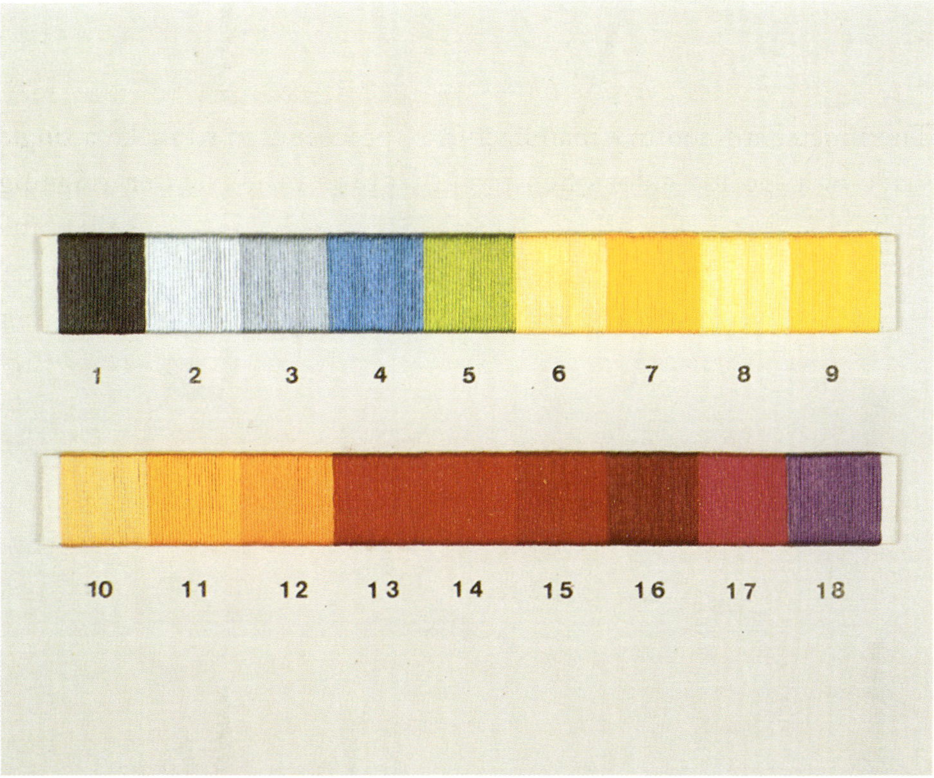

Plate 3 SILK COLORS

1. Black
2. Light Blue (Pale Blue)
3. Blue
4. Dark Blue
5. Green, Grass Green
6. Gold
7. Golden Yellow
8. Light Yellow
9. Yellow, Lemon Yellow
10. Light Orange, Pale Orange
11. Orange
12. Dark Orange, Tippet Colored
13. Scarlet
14. Red Claret, Deep Red
15. Ruby, Crimson
16. Claret, Dark Claret
17. Magenta
18. Violet, Purple

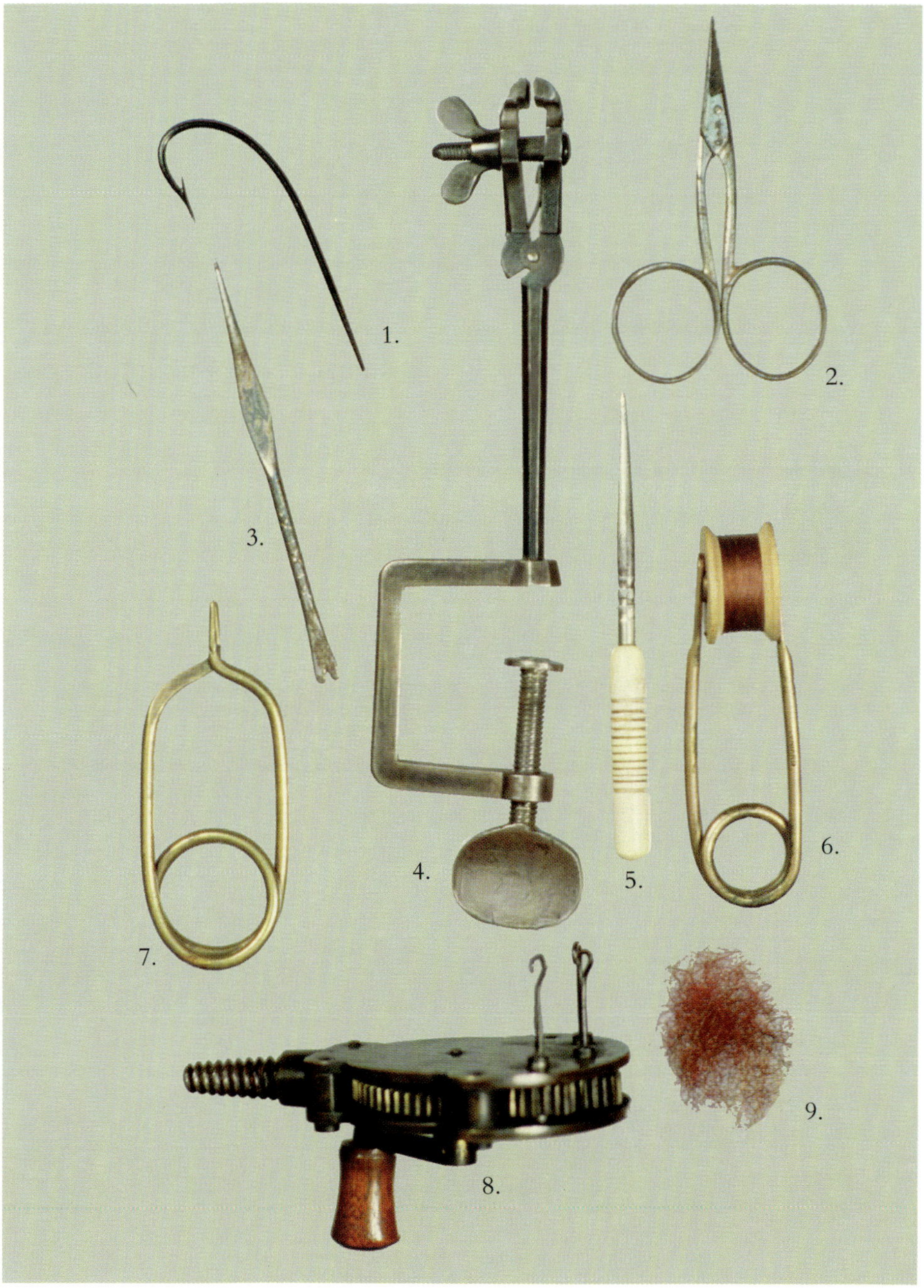

Plate 4 ANTIQUE TOOLS

1. Tapered-Shank Hook
2. Scissors
3. Dubbing Needle Made from Darning Needle
4. Handmade Vise
5. Ivory-Handled Stiletto
6. Bobbin
7. Hackle Pliers
8. Gut-Twisting Machine
9. Pig's Wool

"lemon." In the appendix of the same volume, however, the instructions call for "golden yellow." Even more uncertain are just which shades are meant when the tag of the Black Doctor calls for lemon, and the middle joint of the body for a Popham "lemon yellow." Is there a difference?

Still another color from Pryce-Tannatt's book that will cause a twinge is lilac. The shade of lilac used in the Orange Parson (pictured in Pryce-Tannatt's color plates) is not the same as the lilac on today's color charts. What was "lilac" to Pryce-Tannatt is identified on contemporary charts as violet. Lilac is at least one shade lighter, and when the two shades are placed side by side, the difference is evident.

And just what shade is Green Highlander green? It's often described today as a "hot" or "fluorescent" color. In books that are common references for the dressing of the Green Highlander, the green material may be seal fur, silk, or feathers, and the dressings will read "green" or "dark green." One goes so far as to say "dark green like the color of grass." Pryce-Tannatt listed the proper color as "bright green." Lacking a consensus on just what Green Highlander green is, surely we can answer the question by examining antique examples of the pattern. If these old flies are to be trusted, then we're not even close to using the proper shade of green when we tie these flies with what is today called "Green Highlander green." In my opinion, the correct shade to use is either grass green or plant green. See the Green Highlander in plate 8 for what I believe to be the correct shade of green to use in this pattern.

The most elusive color of all is *golden olive*. Friends in Scotland tell me it had reached a point where articles were being written trying to describe in words just what this color looked like. Fortunately, there is an excellent picture of the fly pattern of the same name on plate VIII of Pryce-Tannatt's book. The most striking characteristic is the lack of much green, usually evident in all shades of olive. If asked to describe the color *golden olive,* one might reply, "A dirty yellow with a hint of green in it."

I present this chapter not to criticize the early writers, but merely to analyze the uncertainties that now exist due primarily to the changes in color technology. Our early writers left us the wonderful legacy of their books on fishing and fly-tying. From studying these books we know that standardized colors did not exist then—nor do they exist today. There are no absolutes. This uncertainty is an inherent part of our hobby, and one that must be viewed with benevolence. It is simply one of the many challenges that building classic Atlantic salmon flies presents to us today.

Colors for Contemporary Tyers

Because of the uncertainty surrounding the colors of silk used in the classics, and recalling the expression "There is nothing new in fly-tying, only that which has been forgotten," I decided to look for a new source of silk flosses. My aim was to find colors that would match, as closely as possible, such colors as puce, claret red, and "tippet-color." I was fortunate to find a splendid line of silks at a local embroidery and yarn shop. Armed with a color chart of all the shades available, and after many hours of comparing, choosing, and a few good-natured arguments, I came up with some surprising results. Just 18 colors from the 112 available would satisfy most of the dressings in our three classic tying manuals (Kelson, Hale, and Pryce-Tannatt).

With so much mystery surrounding the colors in early publications, I had little choice but to start over with new names for available silks. For the most part, these color names have been modified from the old ones to agree with those listed by Hale, Kelson, and Pryce-Tannatt. Please note, then, that my list will show some unchanged names, some similar names, and a few entirely different names.

Let us concede that one particular color can be, and often is, called by several different names. This is undoubtedly why Pryce-Tannatt listed his ten colors of silk *by number,* and then called, *by name,* for some twenty colors in his dressings.

The eighteen colors in plate 3 will meet all of those required for Pryce-Tannatt's dressings, and nearly ninety percent of those colors called for by Kelson and Hale.

Chapter Four

Metallic Tinsels

The flash of tinsel is one of the hallmarks of a salmon fly, yet the sizes and nomenclature of tinsels are confusing. There is no end to the variety of names used to identify the different tinsels—some types have several names—and reference books are often in disagreement regarding the terminology. Such confusion probably originated when the manufacturer's name for a particular tinsel was adopted by some writers and not by others.

Compounding the problem is the fact that the designations for tinsel sizes have their own disorder. Some, although sized by number, are commonly described only as extra-fine, fine, medium, et cetera.

Historically, tinsels were acquired from the garment trade. In fact, Taverner recommends tyers to seek out a Masonic tailor, "of which there is sure to be one in most large cities." Whether there were manufacturers in Taverner's time who produced tinsels exclusively for the fly-tying trade is unknown, but it is a safe assumption that the tinsels used on flies were first borrowed from uniform makers.

Today there are six varieties of tinsel in general use for fly-tying:

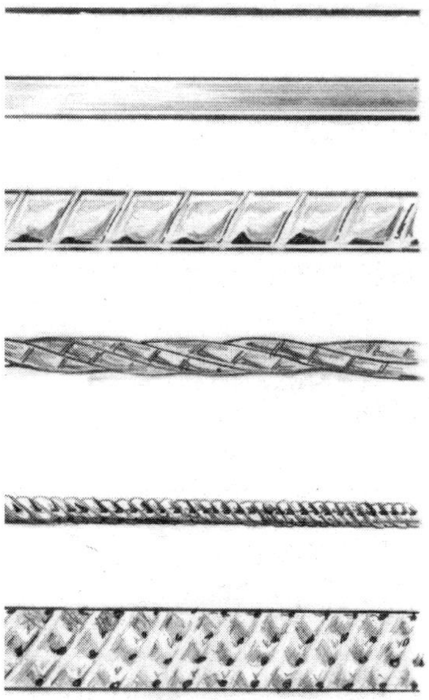

FIGURE 4-1. ILLUSTRATION OF VARIOUS TINSELS

thread (wire), flat, oval, twist (thread), lace (twist), and embossed. These come in various widths, and are either silver- or gold-plated. Silver is more often called for in salmon fly dressings.

THREAD (WIRE)

Hale lists thread as *fine wire,* Kelson calls it *solid wire,* whereas Pryce-Tannatt writes that threads are round, rather than oval, in cross-section.

FLAT

Hale correctly describes flat tinsel as very thin sheet metal that has been cut into strips of various widths. Kelson simply refers to it as tinsel, and says that it was manufactured by flattening solid metal wire. Pryce-Tannatt writes that flat tinsel is fine strips of silver or silver gilt. Close examination of antique flies indicates that flat tinsel did indeed come in sheets, and that each tyer was required to cut the width of tinsel necessary for the fly being dressed.

Oval

Hale describes oval tinsel, correctly, as made of a solid silk core, wound around with very narrow flat tinsel. Kelson lumps oval in with flat and usually calls both simply "tinsel," although occasionally he refers to "flat worm," which he says is made in the same manner as twist tinsel. Pryce-Tannatt says that oval tinsel "consists of a core of floss-silk round which very fine gold or silver wire, has been closely bound by machinery." He doubtless meant very fine *flat* tinsel, for none of his dressings calls for wire.

Twist (Thread, Round)

Twist seems to be the most confusing of the six types of tinsels because of the differing terminologies used to describe its manufacture. Kelson describes twist as "floss silk covered with fine wire" (and goes on to use the word interchangeably with "thread"). Pryce-Tannatt writes, "Two or more strands of an ordinary hempen rope constitute what is known as twist." Much of the confusion results from the fact that twist does indeed look a great deal like fine solid wire, and it is round in appearance.

Lace (Twist)

Hale writes that "cord or lace is two or three threads of twist twisted together so as to form one thick strand." Kelson describes lace as "compound 'twist's—i.e. three lengths twisted together." Pryce-Tannatt omits the term *lace* altogether and calls it twist.

Embossed

Embossed is by far the easiest of our six types to explain, and Pryce-Tannatt does it very well when he writes, "Embossed tinsel . . . as its name indicates, is just embossed flat silver tinsel."

However, there is still more mystery ahead trying to sort out just what type of tinsel each author used in a particular pattern.

Although Hale provides the most accurate descriptions of the types of tinsel, most of his dressings call for silver or gold tinsel for the tags or ribbings without specifying the precise types to use. Very occasionally his dressings call for lace or oval tinsel for ribbing, which leaves us wondering if he intended the tyer to use flat or twist for the tag, and flat ribbings if he did not specify another type. Consequently, I use extra-fine oval tinsel for tips and tags and oval tinsel for ribbing (unless the dressing specifies some other type).

Kelson, on the other hand, was most specific in preferring twist (round) tinsel for most of his tags. If we remember that he refers to both flat and oval as simply "tinsel," it is probably safe to assume that he intends the tyer to use flat tinsel for ribbings unless he specifies a particular type (usually identified in parentheses in his dressings). An example is found in his dressing for the Dunkeld: "Body, gold tinsel; Ribs, gold tinsel (oval)."

Pryce-Tannatt specifies either tinsel or thread for tags. This "thread" would be twist, and the "tinsel" would be flat. The majority of his dressings are specific in calling for types of tinsel for bodies and/or ribbings. Pryce-Tannatt also preferred all-tinsel tags in many of his dressings as, for example, in his Green Highlander. In their dressings for this same fly, Hale calls for silver tinsel and canary floss, while Kelson specifies silver twist and canary floss.

There is one more choice regarding tinsels confronting today's tyer—that of the correct size to use on a given pattern and hook. While no rules are written in this regard, simple judgment and the tyer's eye will usually produce satisfactory results. The photographs in this book will serve as a guide.

Tinsel Types and Terminology

	Name given by				
PHYSICAL DESCRIPTION	HALE (ALCOTT) 1892	KELSON 1895	PRYCE-TANNATT 1914	OTHER REFERENCES TO PRESENT	COMMON USAGE PRESENT
A. Solid round wire, generally fine.	Fine Wire	Solid Wire	No Reference	Wire	Wire
B. Light floss around which is wrapped a fine flat tinsel. Product is round in cross-section.	Twist	Twist	Thread	Round	Thread
C. Light floss around which is wrapped flat tinsel. Product is oval in cross-section.	Oval	Oval Tinsel	Oval	Flatworm	Oval
D. A ribbon of gold or silver metal. Made by flattening solid wire or (archaic) by cutting strips from flat sheets.	Flat	Flat Tinsel	Flat	Plate	Flat
E. Three strands of "B" above, twisted together, like rope, to form one thick strand.	Lace	Lace	Twist	Cord	Twist
F. Flat tinsel that has a pattern raised on its surface.	Embossed	Embossed	Embossed	Embossed (Scotch or English)	Embossed

Except when flat tinsel is used for a tag (tip), extra-fine oval tinsel seems to be the choice of contemporary tyers, rather than twist or thread, although the latter is useful on very small hooks. In full-length tinsel bodies calling for just one type of tinsel ribbing (usually flat or oval), an excellent rule of thumb is to have the amount of body showing—either tinsel or floss—equal to three widths of the ribbing. (This is diagrammed in figure 6-3 in chapter six). Therefore, when the size of the fly is reduced, the tinsel size should be adjusted accordingly. In jointed bodies, the tinsel size will also have to be reduced, or occasionally the type of tinsel will have to be changed. For example, the black-floss portion of a size 4/0 Jock Scott would look very well dressed with extra-fine lace and very narrow flat tinsel. A size 2 Jock Scott, on the other hand, looks best if either the flat or lace is eliminated, and only one tinsel is used. It is important not to obliterate the body material with the ribbing.

Because of their superior quality, and also because they are traditional, the best tinsels to use are those made from silver- and gold-plated copper. These are far superior to Mylar, which is too thin and will stretch. Genuine French tinsel is the best quality, and it is available from some tackle shops that sell fly-tying materials. Occasionally a spool of antique French tinsel will show up. Many are labeled *Vernie,* which means it is varnished to prevent tarnishing. The term is not, as is sometimes thought, a manufacturer's name.

CHAPTER FIVE

Types of Wings

The subject of greatest confusion for contemporary tyers attempting to understand the evolution of featherwing salmon flies seems to be the various types of wings and their construction. This confusion was created by the early writers, who often used different names to describe the same fly-dressing technique. This chapter will explain the major differences in the various wing types described by earlier writers and how they have evolved up to the present, so that contemporary tyers can choose the style of wings they prefer for their own flies.

STRIP WINGS

Pryce-Tannatt referred to this type of wing as a "simple strip wing." This style is similar to that of trout wet flies, and consists of single strips of a particular kind of feather, such as mottled turkey or bronze mallard. Because of their simplicity, strip-wing flies are generally not regarded as classics. One exception is the Thunder and Lightning (see chapter eight). Technically it is a strip-wing. Due to its fame as a salmon fly, however, many tyers consider it a classic pattern.

Whole Wings

Whether or not a pattern fits the whole-wing category depends on whose book is referenced. Taverner lists six distinct ways of winging salmon flies. He defines a whole wing as one incorporating entire feathers back to back[2], such as golden pheasant tippets in the Ranger series. He also classifies wings of peacock herl, peacock swords, and golden pheasant toppings (crests) as whole-feather wings.

Pryce-Tannatt, on the other hand, excludes the Beauly Snow Fly and two others from the whole-wing category and classifies them as *herl wings*. He also creates a separate category for *topping wings,* which are made with golden pheasant crests, tied in one on top of the other. Two earlier books also place herl wings and topping wings in separate categories.

Accordingly, today we define whole-wings as patterns using whole feathers back to back. Three of the twelve flies shown in the color plates accompanying chapter seven—the Durham Ranger (plate 6), the Lady Lillian (plate 11), and the Orange Parson (plate 12)—are whole-wing flies.

Original Mixed Wings

Except for the works of Hale and Kelson, nineteenth-century books have limited instructions on fly-tying. In his *Rod and River,* Major A.T. Fisher writes that "the wings are composed of strips of various feath-

2. The bright ("good") side of a feather is convex as you look at it; the dull side is concave. The term "back to back" means having the dull (concave) sides facing each other.

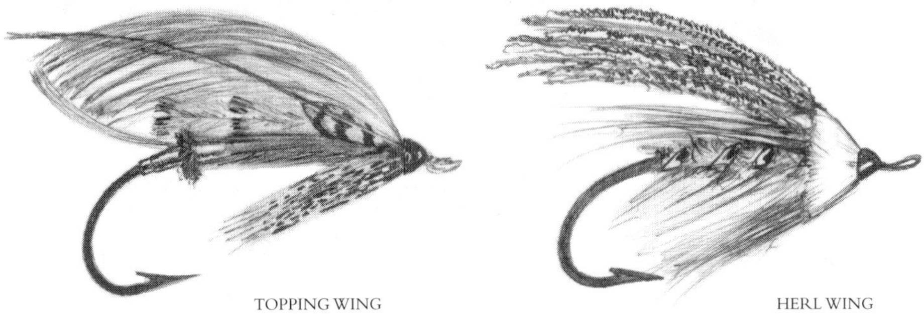

TOPPING WING HERL WING

FIGURE 5-1

ers, placed above, and over each other. The underwing so to speak, veiled by the upper *[sic]*." Francis Francis basically duplicates Fisher's instructions: "If they [the wings] are to run in slips of fibres, cut the slips from feathers out of right and left wings if possible, and they will lie and show better. Lay the slips upon one another on either side . . ." This demonstrates that overlapping wing strips was one of the accepted methods of making wings.

This way of building wings, along with mixing individual fibers singly or in strips and strands, together constituted the broad category known as "mixed wings" until later nineteenth-century tyers and writers started developing more specialized types of wings and brought about some redefinitions of terms.

Mixed Wings or Built Wings?

A full discussion of mixed wings would involve more detail than a chapter allows, but if we stay with three of the most popular books—Hale, Kelson, and Pryce-Tannatt—we can sort out mixed wings. It's important to know that the term *mixed wing* was used by writers long before these three authors published their works. Until the late nineteenth century, all flies, other than a few exceptional types, were generally known as mixed-wings; as a descriptive term, it reflected the widespread use of unmarried individual barbs or strips in wings.

Once Kelson named his wing of individual married fibers a "mixed wing," however, the accepted meaning of the term began to change. It is true that Kelson must be credited for introducing a particular kind of mixed wing. Hale's introduction of his version of the mixed wing using single strands *(following)* gave an additional push to the reclassification of many of the flies once called mixed-wings into a new category called *built-wings*.

Kelson's instructions for making a built wing are difficult to understand. Where other writers give a few paragraphs or a page or two of explanation, his book has seven pages of advice on how to make built wings. Further confusing the issue is the inconsistency of his terminology; he sometimes refers to those same wings as "mixed wings." Nevertheless, the overall point of his text is that built wings consist of married strips, whereas mixed wings are individual fibers married together. An examination of the fly illustration in his book shows that his built wing is made of married strips.

Pryce-Tannatt presents a somewhat contradictory summary of a built wing. He instructs the reader to build the wing in stages and then tie the stages in, one above another, like slates on a roof. The portions underneath are left partially exposed by those immediately above them. In the photographs of flies in his book, however, none of the wings is made of these slate-like portions. Non-overlapping married strips make up one wing, and the wings are tied in, back to back. This is the style of wing used in the color plates in this book of the Black Dose, Green Highlander, Jock Scott, Lady of the Island, Parson, Silver Doctor, and Rosy Dawn (see plates 5, 8, 9, 10, and 13–15). Among contemporary tyers, this latter type of wing and the whole wing are the most commonly used wing types.

Eric Taverner explains his version of built wings as follows: "The materials are tied in successively, the last installment partially embracing [covering] the attached feathers [tied in] during the preceding stage and thus allowing them to be seen." He adds that Pryce-Tannatt describes the effect as being like the partial overlapping of slates on a roof. Later, in his instructions for tying a Jock Scott, Taverner writes:

"The system . . . of constructing a built wing is in my opinion, far too complicated and cumbrous to warrant all the troubles expended. I have, therefore, given up tying in mixed sheathes in three installments and instead marry all the fibres into a single pair of wings." This is the type of wing I build, shown in the color plates of built-wing flies named in the preceding paragraph.

The term *built wing* apparently did not appear in print until the 1880s or 1890s. Assuming that Hale and Kelson used this phrase to distinguish their versions of mixed wings from what was previously recognized as a mixed wing, we can assign models. Hence, the term *built wings* encompasses two methods of construction:

1. Married strips made into a left and right wing, without overlapping sections.
2. Married strips made into sections that overlap preceding sections, much like slates on a roof.

For both types, the usual procedure is to have the wings overlap any underwings given in the dressing, as shown in the Jock Scott, plate 9. Married strips that overlap preceding wing sections appear to have fallen out of favor at the beginning of this century. Today, built wings are constructed as demonstrated in figure 7-25.

Mixed Wings

Hale describes two methods for making mixed wings. His first method uses single strands (barbs) from each feather called for in the dressing for the wing. He tells us to take any strand, lay it "on its back" (a term that Hale did not explain) on the table, and then take another strand and lay it, also "on its back," alongside or on top of the first strand; then take another strand, and so on. Do this until you have formed strips of fibers. He also cautions us not to have any two fibers of the same kind next to one another. "If fibres cross over one another, that's not a problem, as long as they are all from the same side of the parent feather." After several of these strips have been made, they are married into one broad strip. The points of each strip are a little longer than those of the strip below it. The opposite wing is made up the same way. After the broad strips are tied in, some feathers are tied on over them to keep the fibers together in the water. Hale also writes that wings can be varied considerably. "Strips and strands can be mixed, and a right and left wing tied on together; or inner or outer wings composed of strips and strands, like the upper part of a built wing, can be placed together, and the whole tied on at once."

Hale's second method consists of building wings using strips of different feathers. The "primary feather" (which he does not define) is tied on top of the hook. On top of that are tied strips of swan or goose dyed different colors—it does not matter if they are rights or lefts. On top of these are tied narrower strips of different colors. This wing is essentially a bundle of different types of feathers that are tied in around the top and sides of the hook in no particular order.

In appearance both of these wing styles look like elaborate paintbrushes with their bright colors of single barbs and strips bunched together.

In contrast to Hale's manner of construction, the Kelson method is a mixed wing of married fibers. The primary difference between the two is that Hale did not marry individual fibers in a specified order, whereas Kelson did. Kelson's method was to take individual fibers of each type of feather in the dressing; each fiber was in the same order in which it was specified in the dressing, and was repeated as many times as necessary to make the required number of strips. Each strip was then married, each a bit longer than the one preceding it. He refers to the strips as *skins.* The skins married together made the whole of what he also calls a skin.

Kelson named this wing of individual married fibers a *mixed wing,* and wrote that he was the pioneer of the system and that it met with the "greatest share of approval and success." What causes confusion is that he applied the term "mixed wing" to his technique, thus appropriating to his specific wing type a term that had previously been applied to original mixed wings of single barbs or strips. Consequently, the occasional modern tyer may have the incorrect notion that a mixed wing is exclusively the *Kelson* type of mixed wing. This type of wing is illustrated in the Gordon (plate 7). The wing style is popular with many present-day tyers, and there is no denying that it makes a beautiful wing, comparable in appearance to a miniature Persian carpet.

Part of the problem in understanding the instructions of Kelson and Hale results from the fact that the illustrations of flies in their books are drawings rather than photographs. With artistic license, it was a simple matter to depict the flies in idealized, perfect form. This is why it is impossible to tie flies that are exact duplicates of those shown in their books. It is also important to remember that Kelson explains five types of wings: whole-feather wings, topping wings (see figure 5.1 in the whole wings section of this chapter), strip wings, built wings, and mixed wings. The point that overshadows all others is his statement that flies could be tied as "a combination of any of the above"!

With its publication, Pryce-Tannatt's *How to Dress Salmon Flies* made a full turn with new instructions for fly-tying. His change to straightforward techniques and substitutions for many of the exotic feathers modernized featherwing salmon flies for the twentieth century. Changes occur in both his tying methods and his choice of materials used for winging flies. Such bold changes in materials may have resulted from the nonavailability of materials restricted by import regulations. Another factor contributing to these changes may have been that Pryce-Tannatt was a self-taught fly-tyer whose intent was to tie flies to catch salmon. Perhaps he thought that tying flies need not follow strictly the guidelines established by earlier writers. Consequently, his book remains important to contemporary tyers, yet at the same time it leaves us with some unanswered questions.

Were it not for the color plates in Pryce-Tannatt's book, we would have a difficult time trying to unravel his sometimes confusing and imprecise terminology. For example, in his lesson for a Jock Scott (built-wing), for the underwing of white-tipped turkey he instructs the reader to use left *strips* for the left wing and vice versa. A few sentences later he says to tie in married *fibers* of dyed swan, bustard, et cetera. Prior to the end of the sentence, this changes to married *strands.* In his subchapter explanation for a mixed wing, he speaks of "mixed wings, which are made up of a number of single strands of various feathers 'married' to each other in one continuous 'sheath.'" The footnote explains that, "strictly speaking, a mixed wing is composed of a number of single strips of several different kinds of feathers."

It appears to me that Pryce-Tannatt uses the terms *fibers, strips,* and *strands* interchangeably.

Equally puzzling are Pryce-Tannatt's indexed dressings for mixed-wings and built-wings. He lists sixteen patterns for mixed-wings, and except for the Sir Richard they have "mixed tippets in strands" for underwings. Five of his six built-wings have strips (I believe *strips* is the best word to use) of white-tipped turkey for underwings. The sixth built-wing, the Butcher, has a pair of tippets back to back, over which is an underwing of golden pheasant sword and teal. Again, from the photos of Pryce-Tannatt's flies, we can see that wings of both types have married strips, and that none is built in the manner he defines as a *mixed wing.* Also, neither type has overlapping strips. This implies that even though his description of mixed wings is similar to Kelson's, his actual tying was a departure from what had previously been the widespread method for making the Kelson or Hale type of mixed wing.

A major question, then, concerns Pryce-Tannatt's use of tippets in strands for underwings. Why did he index the sixteen patterns as mixed-wings? My best guess is that he developed and was introducing his own particular styles of flies. Then, possibly for his own convenience, he called them *mixed-wings.* There is widespread opinion among modern tyers that the patterns in question are technically not mixed-wing flies because the only notable difference between his built-wing and mixed-wing dressings is the underwings. For both groups of flies, the remainder of the wing construction is fundamentally the same.

Despite the unanswered questions with which Pryce-Tannatt's

book leaves us, it may be the most widely used by modern tyers—particularly by tyers working with the classics for the first time. Pryce-Tannatt was with us for eighty-four years, having been born in 1881 and having died in 1965. He lived to see a second edition of *How to Dress Salmon Flies* published in 1948 by A. & C. Black, the original publisher, and it is now in its third edition (also from A. & C. Black).

I have tried in this chapter to explain earlier writers' views on wing types and to reach some conclusions as to suitable contemporary interpretations of the terms. Nevertheless, there are no fixed standards in the art of building classic Atlantic salmon flies. With as many ways as there are to build wings, it's certainly a tyer's choice to follow whichever style he or she prefers.

CHAPTER SIX

Proportions

Experience and a sensitive eye soon will guide the amateur in the choice of hackles proportioned to the fly. Nothing looks worse or betrays so surely the unskilled hand as the display of body hackles too long or shoulder hackles too short.

SIR HERBERT MAXWELL,
SALMON AND SEA TROUT

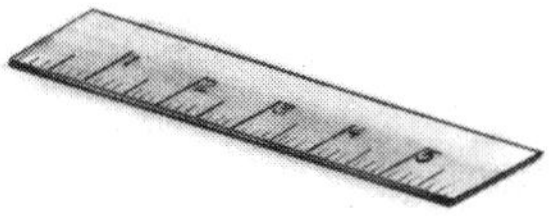

Building featherwing Atlantic salmon flies is made more difficult than it need be due to the lack of written standards for the proper proportions of the individual components of the fly. Beginners and advanced tyers alike find themselves struggling in their attempts to include certain "mysterious" features in their flies. Tyers who are willing to apply themselves purposefully to reading, observing, and research will find that proportions are not that elusive.

Proportions are the relationship between quantities of materials such that if one varies, then the others vary in a manner dependent on the first. An example is measuring the tip of the tail (crest) for proper length and positioning it so that the topping crest, when tied in, will meet the tip of the tail. This is to say that the tail or crest can be either too long or too short. This applies to other parts of a fly as well.

A near synonym for proportion is *symmetry,* which is the harmonious arrangement of parts to reveal their beauty. For a fly to have symmetry, there must be equivalence in the sizes of the individual parts of the fly—and in particular among the components of the wings and wing veiling. An example is a fly that has wood duck and teal as a wing veiling. Both sides of the veiling should be exactly the same in width and length.

Except for Pryce-Tannatt's *How to Dress Salmon Flies,* nineteenth- and early twentieth-century books on fly-tying lack clear, precise explanations of proportions. Little attention was given to describing the relationship between the parts of a fly and its whole.

In the first edition of his book Pryce-Tannatt writes: "The reader will have to try to turn out a Jock Scott as illustrated in figure 91, which is a model of what a well dressed Jock Scott should be. If he succeeds in doing so, he may pat himself complacently on the back, for the proportions and general symmetry are about as near perfection as can be."

It should be noted that the color photographs in Pryce-Tannatt's book did not change from one edition to the next. Similarly, catalogs from Hardy Brothers, one of Britain's leading suppliers of fly-fishing supplies, used the same photographs of flies from the teens into the 1930s. Thus the proportions of the flies shown in both publications remained unchanged from early in the century onward, and for that reason I do not refer to them by dates or editions in this chapter.

Kelson's and Hale's books, which were published earlier than Pryce-Tannatt's, draw no conclusions regarding proportions. While both books have black-and-white plates, Kelson's also has color plates of individual flies that were drawn with artistic license, and the representations of feathers distort their shapes unnaturally. In other words, feathers on birds simply don't grow the way they are illustrated in these plates. Each feather appears to be precisely positioned, giving the flies a mechanical appearance rather than a natural look.

None of this should deter us from including these books in our collections, however. They are valuable for their information on tying techniques and dressings for hundreds of flies.

Regardless of whose photos are viewed—whether Pryce-Tannatt's, Taverner's, or the Hardy Brothers'—there are combinations of features that repeat themselves to the extent that they have established reference points for proper proportions in featherwing salmon flies. A systematic study of the photographs reveals a number of common proportions built into these flies.

Looking at just the main features, we can see the following similarities:

- Floss tags taper, increasing in size as they are wound forward to the butt.
- Body hackles are tied in by their tips, and thereby the barbs increase in length as the hackle is wound forward.
- Throats are at least as long as the longest barbs in the body hackle, and many are a bit longer.
- The height of the wing is equal to the gap of the hook.
- Tips of the crest try to meet the tip of the tail, and most do.
- Wings extend beyond the bend of the hook.
- Heads are blunt and bullet-shaped, and in proportion to the size of the fly.

Proportions are learned from observation and actual measurement of materials with a ruler. To achieve good proportions, the tyer must be consistent in the choice of materials and exercise the discipline to retie a step until completely satisfied with the result. In teaching fly-tying the most difficult lesson to instill is the self-discipline required to redo steps, rather than rushing through in the hope that the fly will look good when it is finished.

Proportions for an Exhibition Fly Tied on a 4/0 Hook

The hook is a Dublin Limerick tapered shank, a favorite because of its graceful bend and delicate barb. (See chapter seven for more detailed information on hooks, as well as a hook chart.)

The tail length and its position are the most important reference points of the entire fly. After they are established, the dimensions of the fly will be secured. Note that the height of the wing and crest (above the body), "A" in figure 6-1, is equal to the gap of the hook. The tip of the tail intersects the wing at its midpoint, "B" in figure 6-1.

Tag

The tip and tag start in back of the point of the barb. Hooks have different barb lengths. If the barb length is shorter than the standard Dublin Limerick barb, the tip will be farther to the left of the shorter barb than is diagrammed below. Letting the tying thread and bobbin hang down from a horizontal hook shank to act as a plumb bob will help establish where the tyer wants to start and stop the tip and

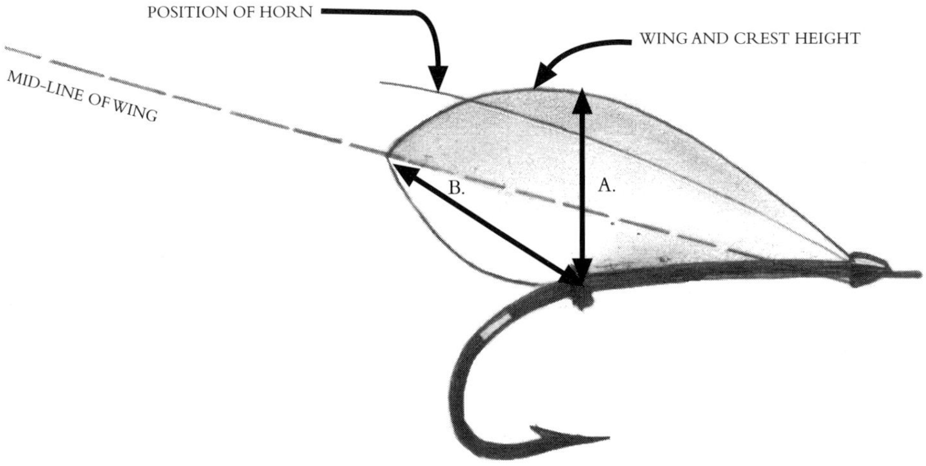

FIGURE 6-1

tag (see figures 7-2 and 7-3 in the following chapter). The widths of both the tip and the tag are left to the discretion of the tyer. However, the butt should not extend beyond the point of the hook as shown in figure 6-1 above. If there is no butt, begin the body at the same position as where the butt would have started—that is, just behind the hook point.

Tail

Measure in a straight line from the tail's tie-in point to its tip. This distance should be one and one-half times the hook gap. For example, a five-eighths-inch hook gap would dictate a tail length measurement of fifteen-sixteenths of an inch. In figure 6-1, the tip of this tail will extend one-quarter of an inch behind the bend of the size 4/0 hook. If this tip of the tail is lower than indicated, the wing will be too long; if it is higher, the wing will be too short.

Butt

Remember that the butt should not extend beyond the point of the hook. For the 4/0 hook in figure 6-1, its width can be three or four turns of herl, making it about one-eighth of an inch wide. Before tying in the butt, cut off all waste ends of the tail and tail veilings as close as possible to the tie-in point. Then the remaining small waste ends are buried under the butt. Burying long waste ends makes it difficult to form a nice body, tapering toward the head.

Underbody

After tying off the butt, wrap the thread forward, stopping one-quarter inch in front of the butt. Tie in a white rayon floss underbody. Bury the waste ends of floss at six o'clock to smooth the underside of the shank. Wrap the tying thread to the right. Stop one-eighth of an inch from the end of the shank, or, in the case of a wire-eye hook, from the end of the straight portion of the shank (see figure 6-2).

Regardless of the technique used to make an underbody, ensure that it has a taper and that your thread ends up exactly in front of the butt.

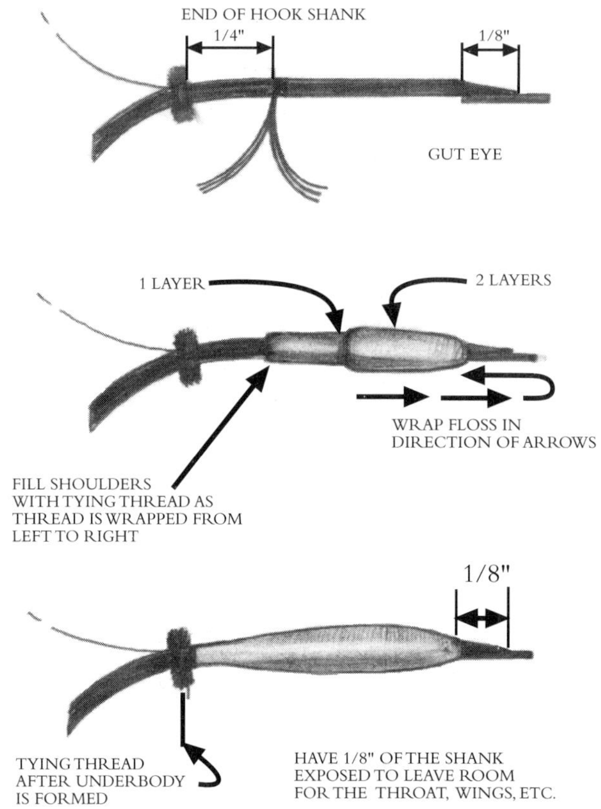

FIGURE 6-2

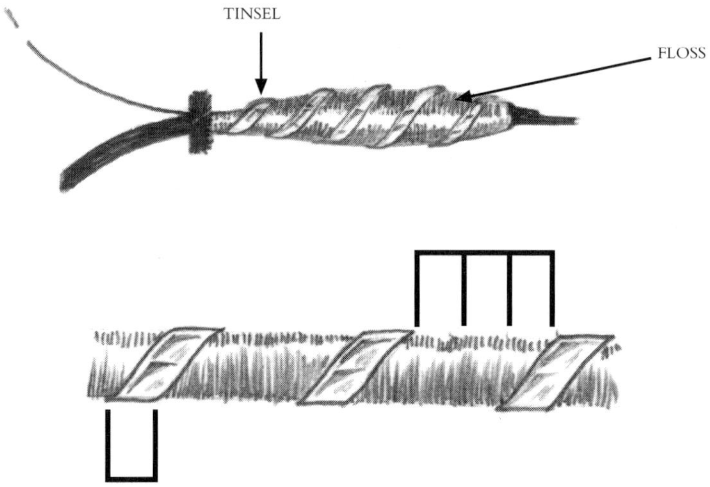

FIGURE 6-3

Ribs

The width of the floss showing between each turn of tinsel should be equal to three times the width of the tinsel. Wrap ribs so that equal amounts of floss show in back of the first turn and in front of the last turn. The tinsel should be secured on the underside of the hook shank at each end. By tradition, a salmon fly always has five turns of tinsel for ribs unless specified differently in a pattern (see figure 6-3).

Body

Build the body in accordance with the dressing. To keep the body smooth, use single strands of silk floss that are untwisted until they are flat. When a dressing calls for a tapered body, the tinsel cannot be wrapped edge to edge and stay together unless a smooth, tapered underbody is first formed.

Body Hackles

Use neck hackles for body hackles. Saddle hackles will usually not produce a pronounced taper from the tie-in point to the throat.

FIGURE 6-4

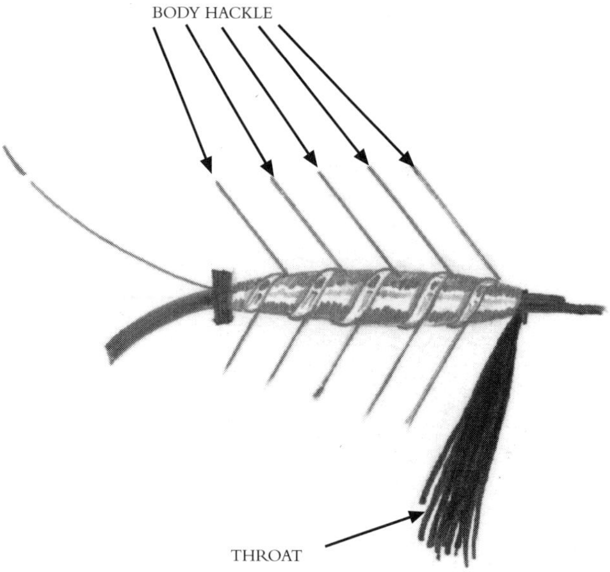

FIGURE 6-5

Throat

Schlappen works well as a throat because of its consistent barb length and smaller quill, which reduces the bulk under the head. The throat should be as long as the longest body-hackle barbs; however, having them a bit longer is the norm (see figure 6-5).

Wings

On a 4/0 fly, for a pattern calling for six different types of feathers, make the individual wing strips about one-eighth of an inch wide. In some other patterns they will have to be narrower or wider, depending on the number of strips in the wing. Marry strips so that the tip of each is exactly the same length. Do not stagger them to come to a point, for they come to a point naturally when applied to the hook. Tie in the wing so that the tip of the wing, at its center, touches the tip of the tail (see figure 6-6).

Wing Veilings

The number of wing veilings in a pattern will determine their individual length. For example, a pattern specifying wood duck, teal, jun-

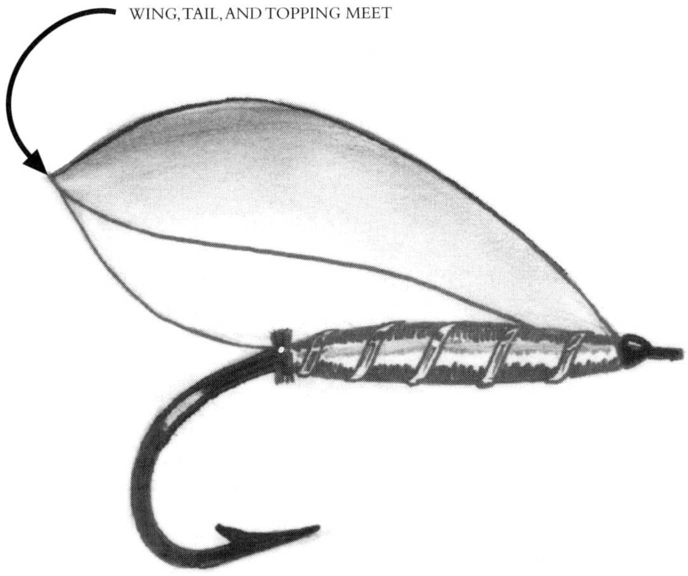

Figure 6-6

gle cock, and kingfisher will have to be tied in to allow the wood duck barring and the tip of the teal to show, then the jungle cock eyes, followed by the full feather of the kingfisher (see figure 6-7). In some patterns the kingfisher is referred to as *cheeks,* which for our purposes can mean either the parts of a wing veiling or the entire wing veiling. (A very early term sometimes encountered is *shoulders,* which generally meant the throat rather than parts of the wing. For simplicity's sake I avoid the term except as it is used in figure 7-28: to indicate the shoulder of the wing.)

Veilings composed of single full feathers, or of the innermost component of a multi-feather veiling (such as the wood-duck-and-teal strip in the diagram), extend back as far as the herl butt. Each successive component is shortened proportionately. For symmetry, make your wing strips of wood duck and teal a bit narrower than two widths of wing strips (which are three-sixteenths of an inch). Some patterns—such as the Orange Parson, the Mar Lodge, and the Popham—call for a single wide strip of wood duck. Its width is left to the discretion of the tyer, but a strip three-sixteenths of an inch wide looks good on a 4/0 fly.

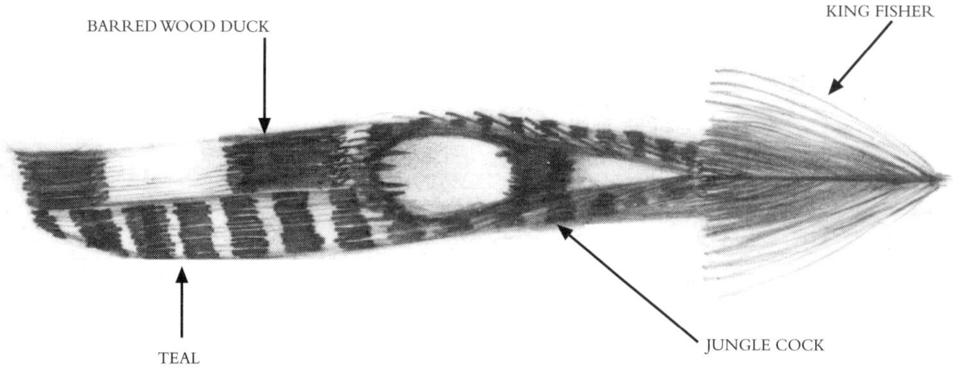

FIGURE 6-7

Crest

After determining the correct length and tie-in point for the pheasant crest, bend the quill to fit the upper edge and contour of the wing.

Horns

Refer to figure 6-1 for the proper proportion of the horns. If they are too long or too high, they become too much of a focal point.

Head

The head should be blunt and bullet-shaped, of a size proportional to the size of the fly. Early writers said to make the heads small, but they didn't say how small. The reason early writers emphasized small heads is that the threads they used were of a much larger diameter than those we have today.

Pattern alone will affect head size. A Jock Scott, for example, has far more materials that have to be secured under the head compared with a Durham Ranger or an Evening Star.

Because proportions were never precisely defined, we must look to published photographs to suggest a standard. Another approach is to obtain contemporary flies that seem to be correct, and to adopt their proportions as your standard.

Don't overlook the basics. Eleven books published between 1816 and 1935 make reference to tapered bodies on salmon flies. Therefore, if that feature is not seen in a fly, it's a safe bet that the fly will have other shortcomings in its proportions.

To clarify why some of the flies in his color plates look jagged, Pryce-Tannatt himself explains: "I am however well aware that the real expert will be able to detect in the colored plates those flies which show undoubted blemishes and perhaps to trace therefrom equally as well as I can, the flies which were dressed nearly two years ago and those which were dressed only a few weeks back." He admits that some are not that well tied; but later on, with practice, they improved. Therein lies the answer to obtaining attractive proportions in a featherwing Atlantic salmon fly.

Study what was done in the past and *practice*.

Twelve Classic Flies and Their Dressings

Black Dose

Durham Ranger

Gordon

Green Highlander

Jock Scott

Lady of the Island

Lady Lillian

Orange Parson

Parson

Silver Doctor

Rosy Dawn

Thunder and Lightning (Irish)

Plate 5 BLACK DOSE

TIP: Extra-fine oval silver tinsel.

TAG: Light orange silk floss.

TAIL: Golden pheasant crest.

TAIL VEILING: Married strips of teal and scarlet swan, back to back.

RIBS: Medium oval silver tinsel.

BODY: First ¼ light blue seal's fur. The remainder is black seal's fur left smooth, not picked out.

HACKLE: Black.

THROAT: Claret hackle.

WINGS: A pair of golden pheasant tippets, back to back. Married strips of scarlet and green swan; light-mottled turkey tail; and golden pheasant tail. Peacock herl along the top edge of and following the contour of the wing.

HORNS: Blue-and-yellow macaw.

HEAD: Black.

Plate 6 DURHAM RANGER

TIP: Extra-fine oval silver tinsel.
TAG: Yellow floss.
TAIL: Golden pheasant crest.
TAIL VEILING: Indian crow.
BUTT: Black ostrich herl.
RIBS: Fine silver lace and narrow flat silver tinsel.
BODY: In four equal sections of golden yellow floss; orange, fiery brown, and black seal's fur.
HACKLE: Badger dyed yellow.
THROAT: A light blue hackle.
WINGS: A pair of jungle cock feathers, back to back, covered for ¾ of their length by a pair of golden pheasant tippets, back to back. These are covered by a shorter pair of tippets reaching to, and covering, the second black bar of the first pair. Jungle cock as a wing veiling.
CHEEKS: Blue chatterer (kingfisher).
CREST: Golden pheasant crest.
HORNS: Blue-and-yellow macaw.
HEAD: Black.

Plate 7 GORDON

TIP: Extra-fine oval silver tinsel.
TAG: Yellow floss.
TAIL: Golden pheasant crest.
BUTT: Black ostrich herl.
RIBS: Fine silver lace and narrow flat silver tinsel.
BODY: First ⅓ yellow silk floss; last ⅔ claret silk floss.
HACKLE: Claret from the yellow silk.
THROAT: Blue hackle.
WINGS: One golden pheasant tippet backed with a golden pheasant sword feather. Peacock herl on the sides, at the bottom of the underwing. Speckled Bustard; light blue, light green, red claret swan; Lady Amherst pheasant tail. Single or double barbs of each type married together repeating themselves until three strips are built. Strips made of single barbs may have to be repeated four times for the proper width of the wing.
WING VEILING: Jungle cock.
CREST: Golden pheasant crest.
HEAD: Black.

Some writers describe this type of wing as a mixed wing, but it is a built wing of married barbs that are repeated to make up married strips.

Plate 8 GREEN HIGHLANDER

TIP: Extra-fine oval silver tinsel.
TAG: Yellow floss.
TAIL: Golden pheasant crest.
TAIL VEILING: Barred wood duck.
BUTT: Black ostrich herl.
RIBS: Medium oval silver tinsel.
BODY: First ¼ yellow silk floss; the remainder is grass green seal's fur.
HACKLE: Grass green over the seal's fur.
THROAT: Yellow.
WINGS: A pair of golden pheasant tippets, back to back. Married strips of yellow, orange, and green swan; florican; peacock wing; and golden pheasant tail. Married strips of teal and wood duck as a wing veiling. Bronze mallard as a roofing.
SIDES: Jungle cock.
CHEEKS: Indian crow.
CREST: Golden pheasant crest.
HORNS: Blue-and-yellow macaw.
HEAD: Black.

Plate 9 JOCK SCOTT

TIP: Extra-fine oval silver tinsel.
TAG: Light (pale) yellow floss.
TAIL: Golden pheasant crest.
TAIL VEILING: Indian crow.
BUTT: Black ostrich herl.
RIBS: Fine oval silver tinsel over the golden yellow floss; fine lace and narrow flat silver tinsel over the black floss.
BODY: In two equal halves. First half, golden yellow floss, veiled above and below with toucan, butted with black ostrich herl. Second half, black floss.
HACKLE: Black over the black floss.
THROAT: Speckled guinea fowl.
WINGS: A pair of black white-tipped turkey tail strips, back to back. Over these, but not entirely covering them, married strips of peacock wing; yellow, scarlet, and blue swan; speckled bustard; florican; and golden pheasant tail. Two barbs of peacock sword feathers along the sides and at the top edge of the wings. Married strips of teal and wood duck as a wing veiling. Bronze mallard strips as a roofing.
SIDES: Jungle cock.
CHEEKS: Blue chatterer (kingfisher).
CREST: Golden pheasant crest.
HORNS: Blue-and-yellow macaw.
HEAD: Black.

Plate 10 LADY OF THE ISLAND

Originated for Bert Fram of Prince Edward Island, Canada, a lady who symbolizes contagious good will toward the world.

TIP: Extra-fine oval silver tinsel.
TAG: Scarlet floss.
TAIL: Golden pheasant crest.
TAIL VEILING: Green parrot (alternative, green swan).
BUTT: Black ostrich herl.
BODY: First ⅔ is green floss; last ⅓ is peacock tail herl.
HACKLE: Green.
THROAT: White and green hackles.
WINGS: Golden pheasant tippets, back to back. Married strips of yellow, white, and green goose; florican; speckled bustard; cinnamon turkey tail. Bronze mallard as a roofing. Jungle cock as a wing veiling.
CHEEKS: Indian crow.
CREST: Golden pheasant crest.
HORNS: Yellow macaw or turkey tail dyed yellow.
HEAD: Black.

Plate 11 LADY LILLIAN

This is an exhibition pattern named for my wife, Lillian, for her understanding of my hobby and to express my appreciation for her support.

TIP: Extra-fine oval silver tinsel.
TAG: Light blue floss.
TAIL: Golden pheasant crest.
TAIL VEILING: Barbs of blue peacock body feathers.
BUTT: Black ostrich herl.
BODY: Magenta floss.
HACKLE: Magenta.
RIBS: Fine silver lace and narrow flat silver tinsel.
THROAT: Claret and light blue hackles.
WINGS: Lady Amherst pheasant tippets, back to back. These are veiled with smaller tippets, also back to back, and extending to the black bar of the larger pair of tippets. Blue peacock body feathers for ⅓ of the length of the wing.
CHEEKS: Kingfisher.
CREST: Golden pheasant crest.
HORNS: Natural black turkey tail or turkey tail dyed black.
HEAD: Black.

Plate 12 ORANGE PARSON

TIP: Extra-fine oval silver tinsel.
TAG: Lilac floss.
TAIL: Golden pheasant crest.
TAIL VEILING: Golden pheasant tippet strands.
RIBS: Medium oval gold tinsel.
BODY: In four equal sections of orange floss, darker orange seal's fur, scarlet seal's fur, and fiery brown seal's fur.
HACKLE: Yellow.
THROAT: Cock-of-the-rock.
WINGS: A pair of golden pheasant tippets, back to back, veiled with cock-of-the-rock. Wide strips of wood duck as a wing veiling.
CHEEKS: Blue chatterer (kingfisher).
CREST: Two or three golden pheasant crest feathers.
HORNS: Blue-and-yellow macaw.
HEAD: Black.

Plate 13 PARSON

TIP: Extra-fine oval gold tinsel.
TAG: Light orange silk floss.
TAIL: Golden pheasant crest.
TAIL VEILING: Blue chatterer (kingfisher).
BUTT: Black ostrich herl.
RIBS: Medium oval gold tinsel.
BODY: Claret floss.
HACKLE: Claret.
THROAT: Blue hackle.
WINGS: Golden pheasant tippet in strands, back to back. Married strips of dark turkey; yellow, red, and blue swan; peacock wing; speckled bustard; and golden pheasant tail. Married strips of teal and wood duck as a wing veiling. Bronze mallard as a roofing. Guinea fowl strips as a wing veiling.
CHEEKS: Blue chatterer (kingfisher).
CREST: Golden pheasant crest.
HORNS: Blue-and-yellow macaw.
HEAD: Black.

Plate 14 Silver Doctor

Tip: Extra-fine oval silver tinsel.
Tag: Golden yellow floss.
Tail: Golden pheasant crest.
Tail Veiling: Blue chatterer (kingfisher).
Butt: Scarlet wool.
Ribs: Fine oval silver tinsel.
Body: Flat silver tinsel.
Throat: Light (pale) blue hackle, followed by widgeon flank.
Wings: Golden pheasant tippet in strands, back to back, over which are wide strips of golden pheasant tail. Married strips of scarlet, blue, and yellow swan; florican; speckled bustard; peacock wing; and light-mottled turkey tail. Married strips of teal and wood duck as a wing veiling. Bronze mallard strips as a roofing.
Crest: Golden pheasant crest.
Head: Scarlet wool.

Plate 15 ROSY DAWN

TIP AND TAG: Extra-fine oval gold tinsel.

TAIL: Golden pheasant crest.

TAIL VEILING: Golden pheasant tippet strands.

BUTT: Black ostrich herl.

BODY: In two equal halves. First half is embossed silver tinsel; second half is medium oval gold tinsel. These sections are butted at the joint with a magenta hackle wound on as a collar and pushed back with one turn of thread.

THROAT: A magenta hackle followed by a light (pale) blue hackle.

WINGS: A pair of golden pheasant tippets, back to back. Married strips of yellow, blue, and scarlet swan; and golden pheasant tail. Jungle cock as a wing veiling.

CREST: Two or three golden pheasant crest feathers.

HORNS: Blue-and-scarlet macaw.

HEAD: Black.

Plate 16 THUNDER AND LIGHTNING (IRISH)

TIP: Extra-fine oval silver tinsel.
TAG: Golden yellow silk floss.
TAIL: Golden pheasant crest.
TAIL VEILING: Indian crow.
BUTT: Black ostrich herl.
RIBS: Fine or medium oval silver tinsel.
BODY: Black floss.
HACKLE: Fiery brown.
THROAT: Jay (alternative: guinea fowl dyed blue).
WINGS: Married strips of yellow, scarlet, and blue swan; speckled bustard; golden pheasant tail. Bronze mallard strips as a roofing.
HORNS: Blue-and-yellow macaw.
HEAD: Black ostrich herl.

CHAPTER SEVEN

Building Classic Featherwings

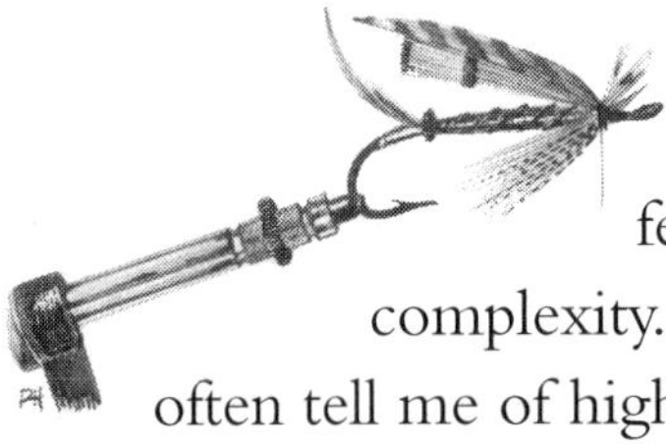

The most important part of building a featherwing fly is not to be intimidated by complexity. The people who coordinate the classes I teach often tell me of highly experienced tyers who are hesitant to participate because they think these flies are too complex. Admittedly the classics are complex, but they are not beyond the capabilities and determination of anyone who wants to become proficient at building them.

Begin by concentrating on and learning the techniques. It is not a matter of simply tying in materials and hoping a fly will turn out well. You have to make it happen, and it will not develop unless specific techniques are used. Throughout this chapter certain methods are presented that were first explained by earlier tyers. Learn techniques from study, from research, and, by all means, from trying your own. Remember to set your own pace. Time should be a commodity. Taverner used the term *Greek Method* for building flies; this means duplicating the fly that is used as a reference. By carefully selecting materials to match as closely as possible those used in the model, it isn't that difficult to copy a study fly successfully. For selecting materials, a shop that supplies salmon fly materials is your best bet, especially if the staff gives customers the opportunity to select personally from their inventory. For example, a shop drawer full of golden pheasant crest and other feathers in large quantities allows you to pick what you think will work best. At the same time, sport shops with diverse inventories are well worth checking out. Occasionally a spectacular type of material becomes available. While you are there, ask for old silkworm-gut leaders for gut-eyed flies. Size and color are unimportant as long as the material is genuine.

Feather quality is an intangible, which doubtless explains why there are virtually no written guidelines on how to identify feathers of sufficient quality for building a salmon fly. Unfortunately, I can do no better than my predecessors, because it isn't possible to give guidelines here that will describe precisely what to look for when selecting materials. Trial and error is the answer. Color, shape, size, and appearance are the determining factors. By all means, study the color plates. I chose the materials used after having built more than fifteen hundred flies. My hope is that the flies in the plates will give you some idea of what to look for when making your choices. There will come a time in your own tying when selecting quality materials will be a simple matter of looking at a particular feather and knowing whether it will work.

Tools and Supplies

My comments on tools will be brief, because tyers who have reached the point of building featherwing salmon flies already will have acquired most of the tools they need.

A vise with a rotating head is not mandatory, but without one, the task of building flies is similar to driving railroad spikes with a tack hammer. As well as having a rotating head, the vise should have interchangeable jaws—one set of which is serrated—that are gapped wide enough to hold large hooks. Some vises are rated to hold size 32 through 10/0 hooks. The HMH vise was my choice in 1982 after disappointing results with an English-made unit with smooth jaws. The

English vise did not exert enough pressure to stabilize large hooks in its smooth jaws.

Additional tools are scissors (both straight and curved), hackle pliers, a whip finisher, tweezers, thread bobbins, and a six-inch ruler.

Some makes of scissors are very expensive; however, for a person new to the art of building flies, a moderately priced pair will get the job done. My preferred hackle pliers have rubber inserts, which grip very well. Tweezers with serrated tips also have a firm hold. The only difference among whip finishers appears to be choice of manufacturer.

A standard bobbin is good for 6/0 threads and up. A bobbin threader/cleaner should also be considered. It is much easier to use one than to try to fish (no pun intended) thread through a tube loaded with wax. Threaders with straight heavy-gauge wire are convenient for cleaning wax buildup from the bobbin tubes. Two other items to include are thread and containers for head cement and liquid wax.

I cannot overemphasize the importance of using prewaxed thread. Unwaxed thread will not hold compressed components when the bobbin weight is released, because the thread does not grip on itself. Another advantage of prewaxed thread is that you don't have to make half hitches or reverse the thread, both of which procedures add unwanted bulk. One to three wraps will hold components in place from the weight of the bobbin alone. Therefore, why take three or four turns of thread if they are not needed? For example, at the butt one turn of thread will hold the ostrich hackle until the tinsels are tied in. After that, the body materials are secured. With the wraps compounded, four turns are holding the butt. The same applies to wool butts. The rule of thumb is to use only as many wraps of thread as are required to hold a component until the next part is tied in.

Danville's 6/0 prewaxed thread—in primrose or white for the bodies and black for the head—answers the call very well. Danville's 6/0 is the only type I use, but there are, of course, other types of thread equally as good. Whatever thread you use should be prewaxed and should have strength for its size. I don't use monocord because it adds too much bulk to the fly—particularly at the head.

For convenience, storage, and ease of application small bottles with built-in applicators for head cement and liquid wax are recommended. It's an absolute necessity to be able to thin both when they thicken. Matarelli applicator bottles are excellent for this purpose. Head cement should have a consistency slightly thicker than water for deep penetration and fast drying. Liquid wax is the opposite. It should be thick, though not to the point that it leaves strings of wax on the applicator.

Pryce-Tannatt's eighty-year-old remark on hooks is still up-to-date when applied to contemporary presentation flies. He wrote: "The purpose of the hook is primarily of course to connect the salmon firmly and securely to the angler. It however, performs another function by varying its relative proportions and thickness of its iron; it has considerable influence upon the practical effect of the pattern dressed on it." Linking effect to appearance, the hook plays a very important part in how a fly will look when it is finished.

Available hook types run a massive gamut. Selection will depend entirely on which type of fly is being built—whether for fishing or for exhibition. Exhibition patterns on tapered-shank hooks are now the accepted tradition, but they can also be built on returned/wire-eyed hooks, and with more ease because this type of hook provides a foundation on which to set wings—a foundation lacking in a tapered-shank hook.

I work exclusively with size 4/0 tapered-shank hooks because this larger size allows all of the components of the pattern to be seen. The recommended size to *practice* on is 2/0 with a wire eye instead of a tapered shank. An added advantage of using 2/0 hooks is the availability of feathers of sufficient size to build wings. Some types of feathers, such as bronze mallard, peacock wing, and teal, that are not large enough can be a problem when working with 4/0 hooks and up. But large feathers of all types are available; it takes a little more sorting of stock to find them.

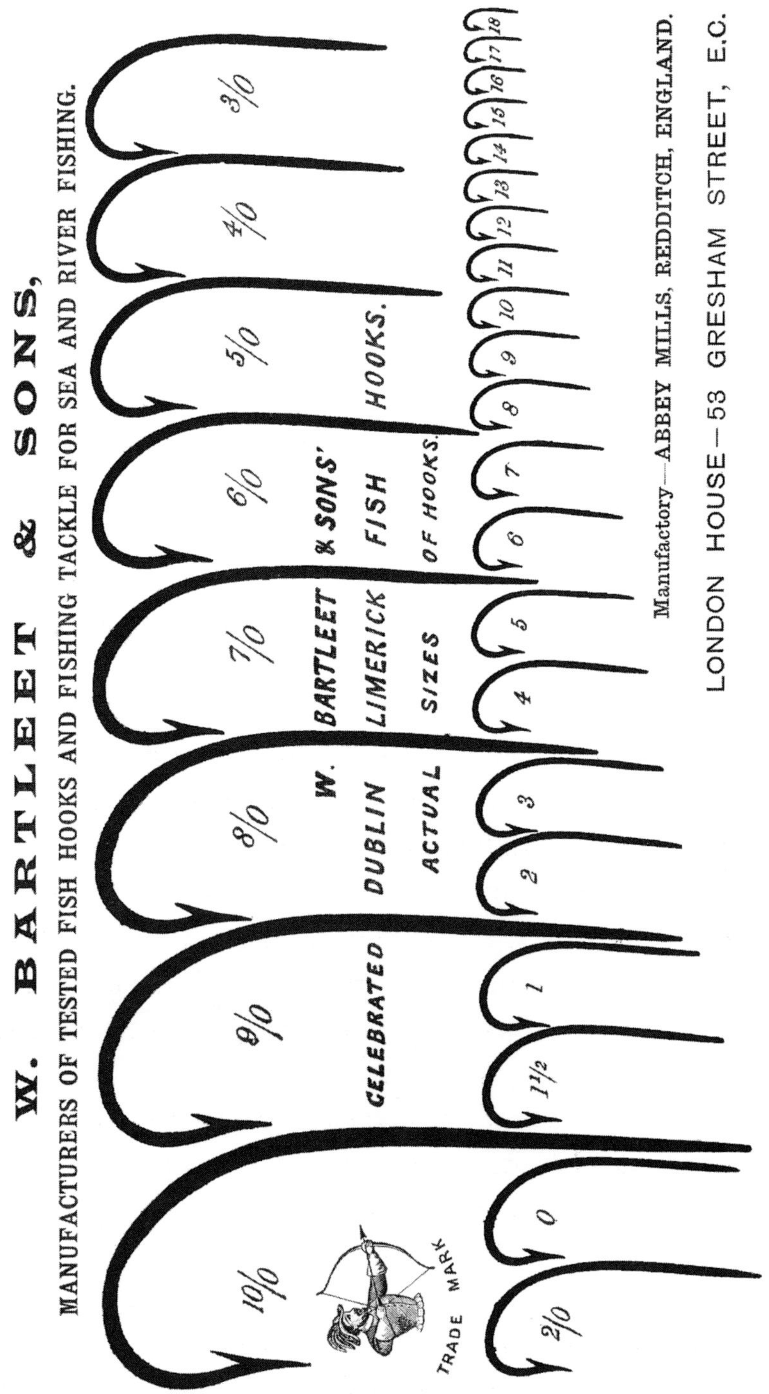

This chart, from an advertisement for Bartleet hooks in the 1892 edition of Hale's *How to Tie Salmon Flies*, provides an accurate guide to hook sizes.

Flies for fishing are another matter. Most are built on hooks smaller than 1/0. Wire size, shank length, bend, and barb length vary considerably among manufacturers. A favorite of mine for fishing flies is a Wilson single with an upturned eye. It has a graceful bend, strong fine wire, and excellent holding power. It is very compatible with the proportions of the bodies and wings of small flies.

Some contemporary hooks will not have the graceful lines of the Dublin Limerick bend, a fact that will affect proportions as they are outlined in chapter six. However, hook styles and proportions do not matter as much in a fishing fly, since it is doubtful whether a salmon gives much thought to even distribution of materials or to hook style in deciding whether to take a fly.

The Building Process

The following are step-by-step instructions and photographs for building five representative classic salmon flies. After completing these five patterns, you should be well prepared to build any of the additional flies whose dressings are listed in chapter eight.

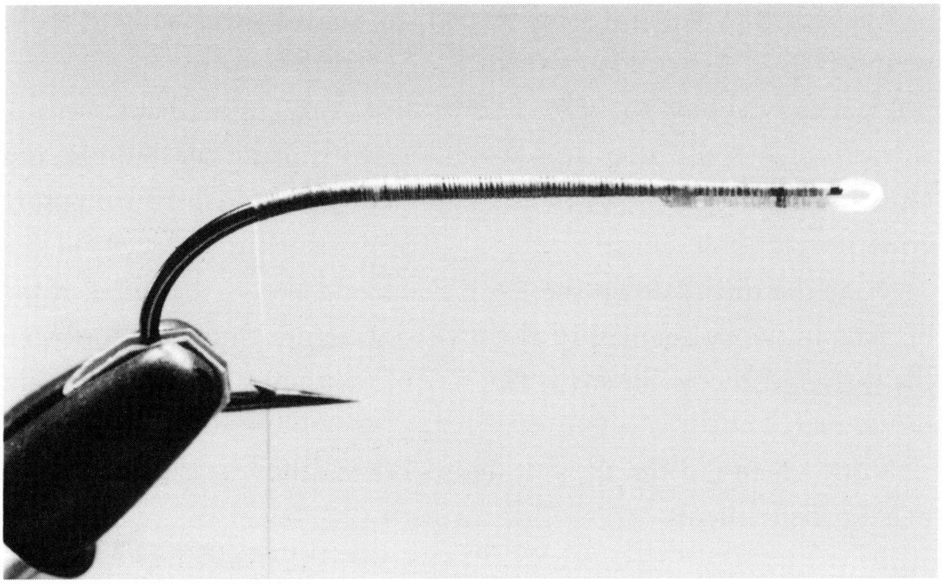

FIGURE 7-1

Parson (plate 13)

FIGURE 7-1

Prepare a 4/0 tapered-shank hook by bending a very slight curve in the shank. Early hooks were manufactured with both straight and curved shanks. A curved shank adds to the overall good appearance of a fly. Also, check the gap and shank length of the hook against the hook scale in this chapter. There are instances of contemporary tapered-shank hooks being made with 6/0 gaps and 4/0 shanks, as well as some with shanks that are 1X or more longer than those shown on scales of standard hook sizes.

Wrap a foundation of 6/0 primrose or white thread ½ inch along the shank of the hook, leaving 1/32 inch of the end of the shank showing. Wrap the gut on at five o'clock on the far side. Bend the gut around the diameter of a shepherd's hook (see figure 7-54) or other small round tool. A ⅛ inch inside diameter of the gut eye is a nice size to have on a 4/0 hook. After forming the eye, wrap the gut in at seven o'clock on the near side. The strands of gut should not be longer than the ½-inch foundation of the thread.

The hook is tilted in figure 7-1 to show how the gut looks wrapped in.

Prior to wrapping the thread down the shank, ensure that the shank is horizontal in the vise. This will allow you to use the bobbin as a plumb bob for locating where to begin or end parts of the fly to ensure good proportions.

Wrap the thread down the hook shank and stop at the point of the hook; spin the bobbin either clockwise or counterclockwise to flatten the thread. After the thread is flat, wrap to within 1/16 inch of the point of the barb.

Note where the thread is in figure 7-1 and how it can be used to make measurements.

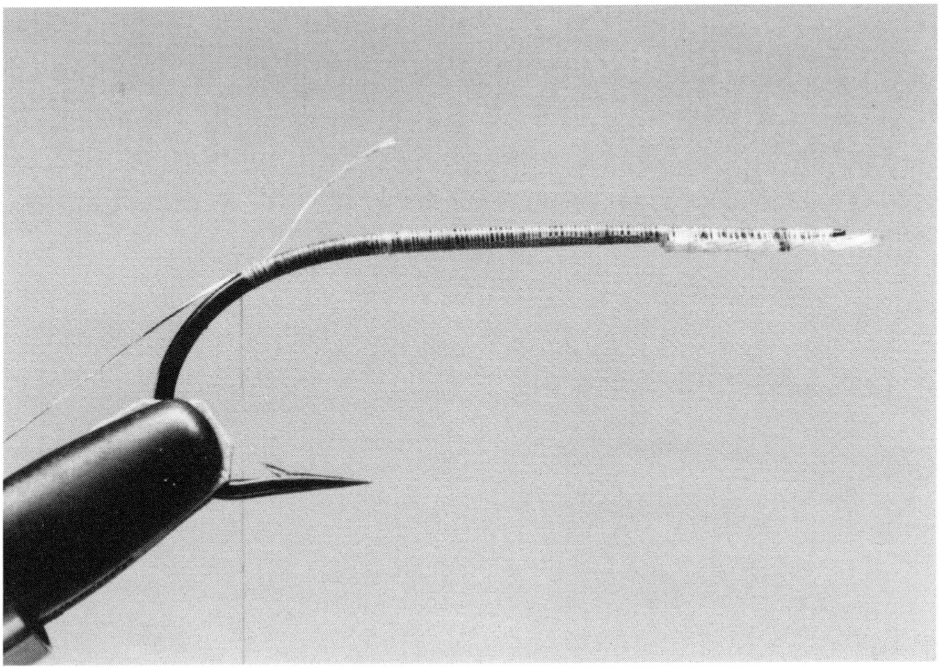

FIGURE 7-2

FIGURE 7-2

This is Hale's method for tying in a tinsel tip: Strip ½ inch of metal off the extra-fine oval gold tinsel. With one turn of the thread, tie in the tinsel core at twelve o'clock on the top of the hook shank. Pull the tinsel to the left until the metal of the tinsel is 1/16 inch to the left of the point of the barb. Wrap the thread to the left until it touches the metal; then wrap the thread back to the right about 1/16 inch. Cut off the waste end of the tinsel core.

Take one turn of tinsel around the bare shank of the hook, followed by six more turns of tinsel to the right for a total of seven wraps of tinsel.

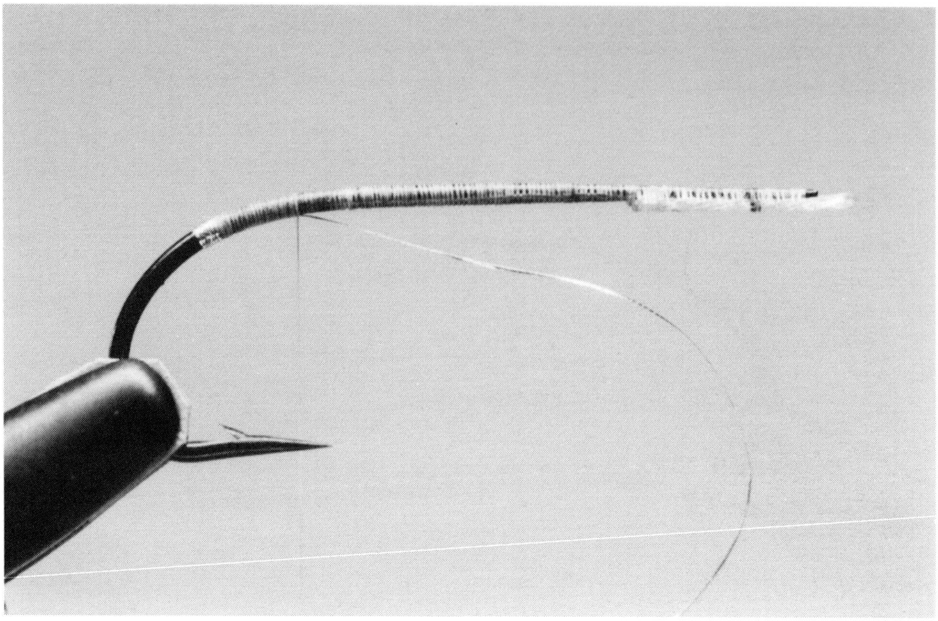

FIGURE 7-3

FIGURE 7-3
Bury the waste end of tinsel under the hook shank at six o'clock. Wrap to the right and stop $\frac{1}{16}$ inch before reaching the point of the hook. Cut off the waste end of tinsel.

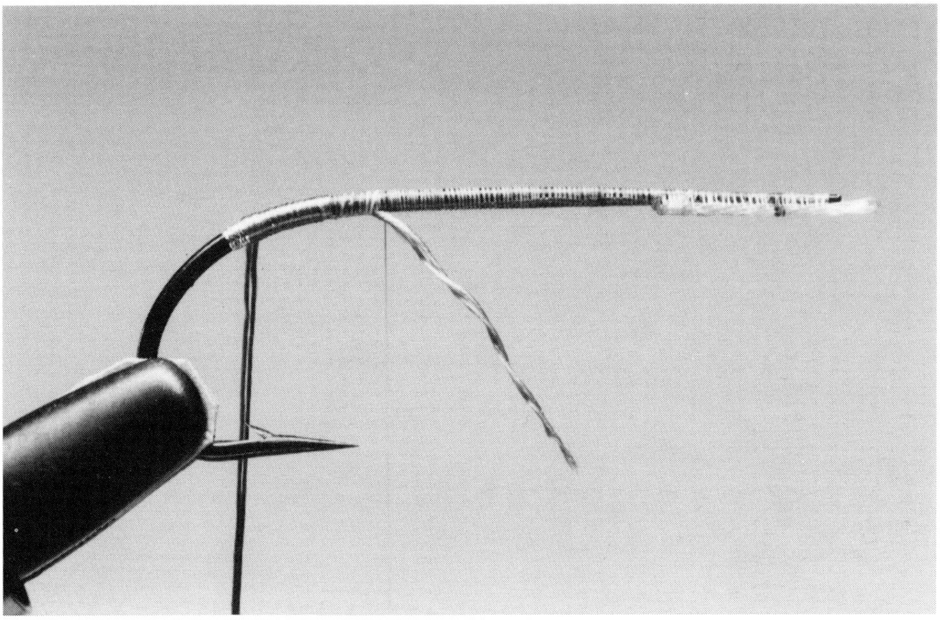

FIGURE 7-4

FIGURE 7-4

Tie in the light orange silk floss at six o'clock; then take five random wraps of thread to the right to hold the floss in place while it is wrapped, edge to edge, down to the tinsel. Thereafter, wrap the floss back to the right to where it was tied in. Hold the waste end of the floss in the left hand. Unwrap the five turns of thread, and tie in the floss with three turns of thread, one on top of the other. Cut off the waste end of floss. The two layers of floss start and stop where it was tied in.

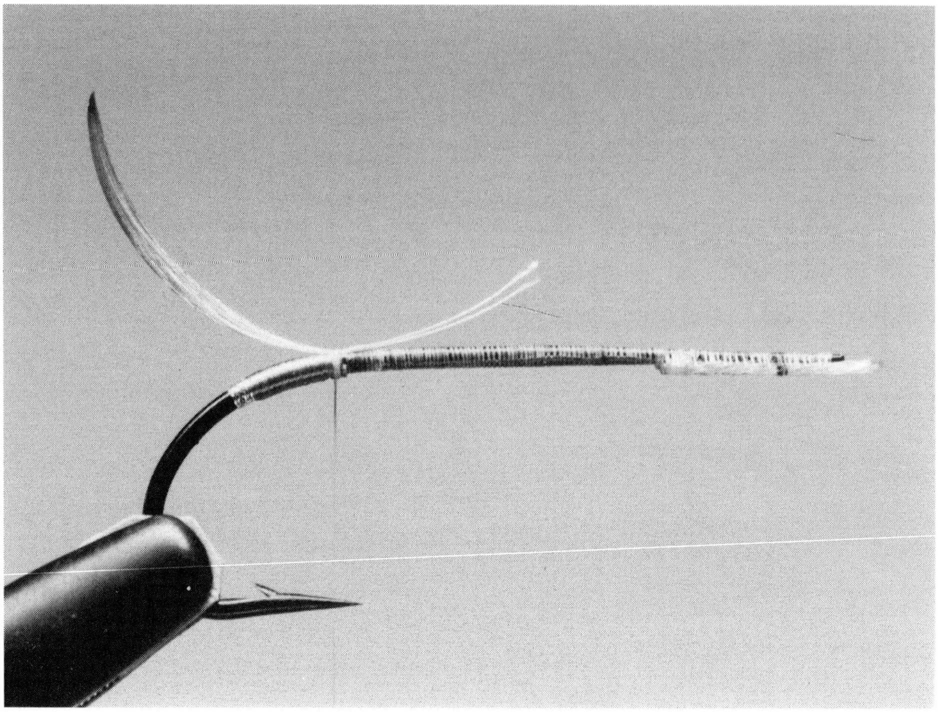

FIGURE 7-5

FIGURE 7-5

Select two golden pheasant crests long enough to equal 1½ times the gap of the hook. Most crests end up crooked from washing and drying. Holding them over a steaming sauce pan will restore their natural shape. To save time, when steaming the crests for the tail, include the long crest for the wing topping as well. Crests that are wet and put on a glass or tumbler to dry will have their barbs matted together.

Strip off the downy barbs at the base of the two feathers. Put one on top of the other with the tips exactly even. Moisten the whole feathers with the tips of your fingers. Tie them in on top of the hook shank at twelve o'clock with three turns of thread, one on top of the other.

For position, length, and measurements, see chapter six.

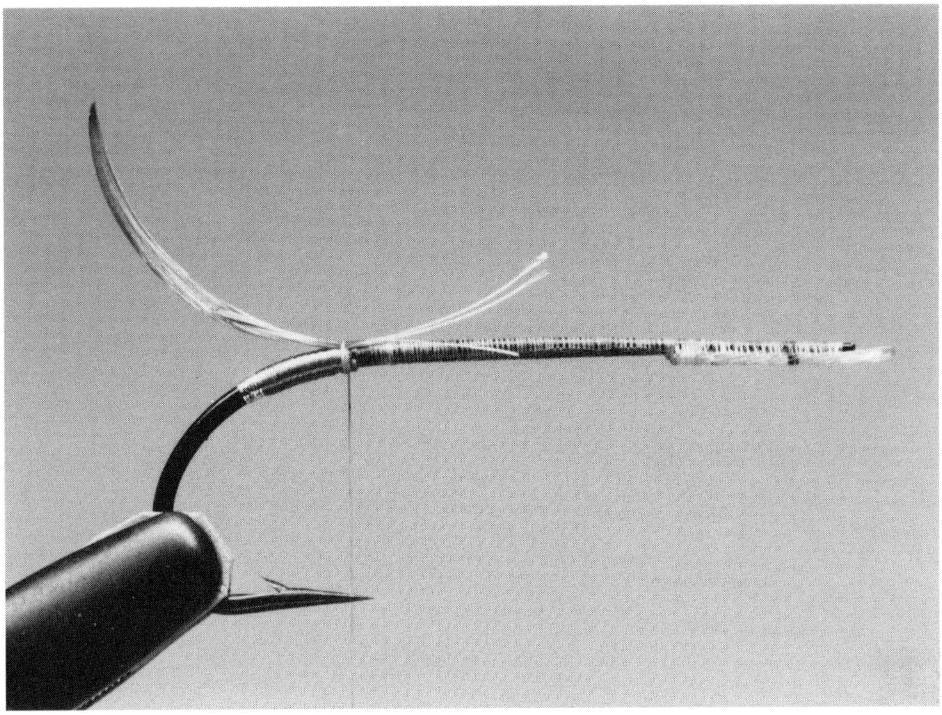

FIGURE 7-6

FIGURE 7-6

Strip off the downy barbs of a kingfisher saddle hackle feather. Moisten the feather and tie it in at twelve o'clock on top of the tail, good (bright) side up. Take two turns of thread one on top of the other, and catch two or three barbs of the feather under the thread. This will prevent the feather from rolling over from thread pressure.

Note that the turns of thread are always one on top of the other, and that there are only enough turns to hold each feather or material as it is tied in. Turns of thread are compounded. Why add unwanted bulk from too many turns of thread? This applies to each step in building a fly.

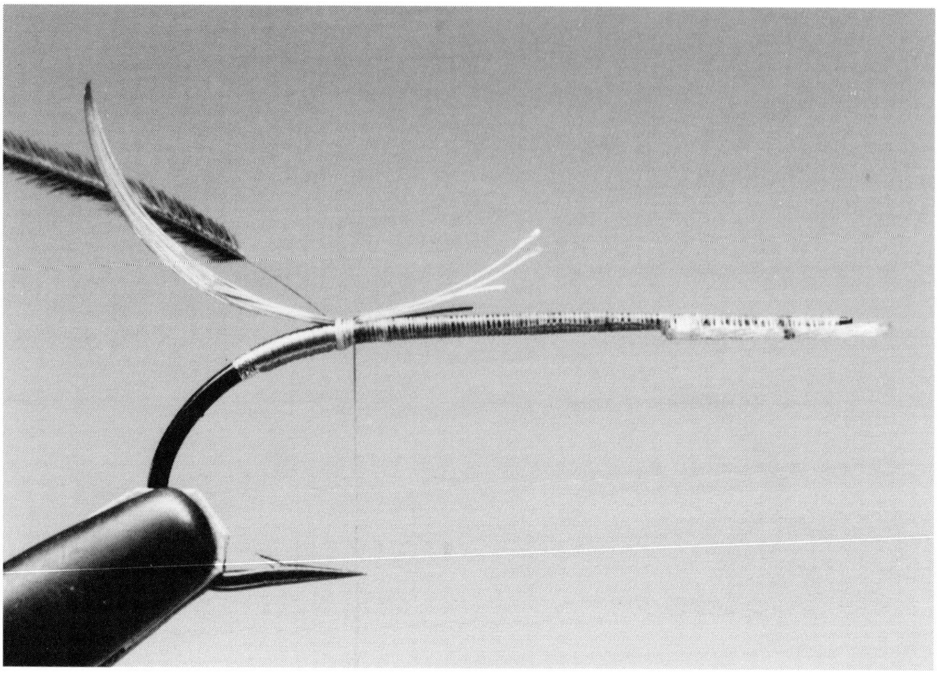

Figure 7-7

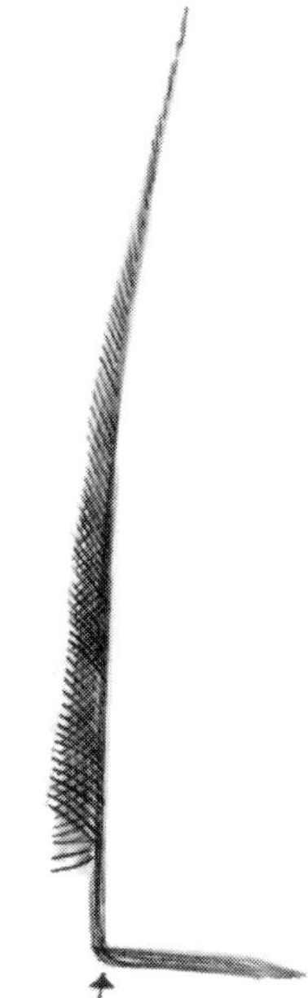

Figure 7-7a

FIGURE 7-7
The width of the butt is not subject to any fixed rules; however, it should cover the waste end of the tail materials, which is its single purpose. For a 4/0 hook, four turns of herl or ⅛-inch width is a usual proportion.

Strip ½ inch of the barbs off the base of a black ostrich herl. Estimate how much of the stripped quill[3] it will take to make one turn around the shank of the hook. At that point make a 90-degree bend in the quill, as in figure 7-7A.

Tie the herl in at three o'clock on the far side, making sure the barbs are pointing toward the rear of the fly. Wrap the thread forward the width of the butt.

Cut off all waste ends as close to the thread as possible. Cutting the waste ends one at a time allows more precise trimming.

3. *Quill* can mean either a whole feather or the shaft of a feather. *Quill*, rather than *shaft*, is the term more widely used in fly-tying, i.e., quill-bodied flies.

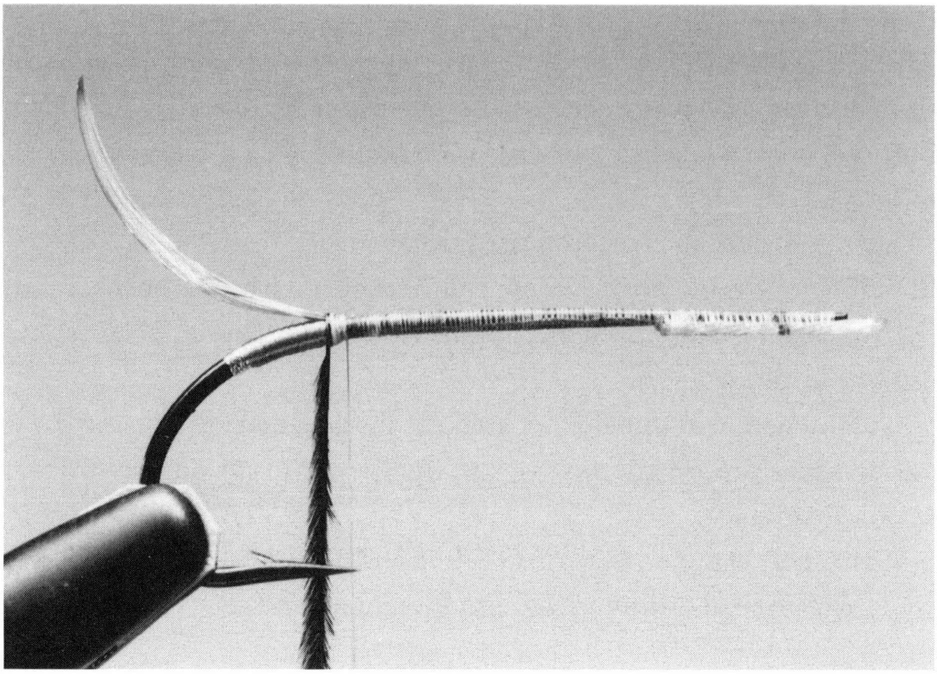

FIGURE 7-8

FIGURE 7-8

Note that the thread is exactly even with the point of the hook. This photo shows the first turn of stripped quill, and the barbs of the herl are facing toward the rear of the fly. The stripped quill acts as a support for compacting the turns of herl. As the herl is wound in, pressure against the stripped quill makes the barbs stand up straight. Tie off the herl with one turn of thread at six o'clock. The weight of the bobbin will hold it in place. Cut off the waste end of herl.

At this point there are no waste ends in front of the butt and the butt is not beyond the point of the hook.

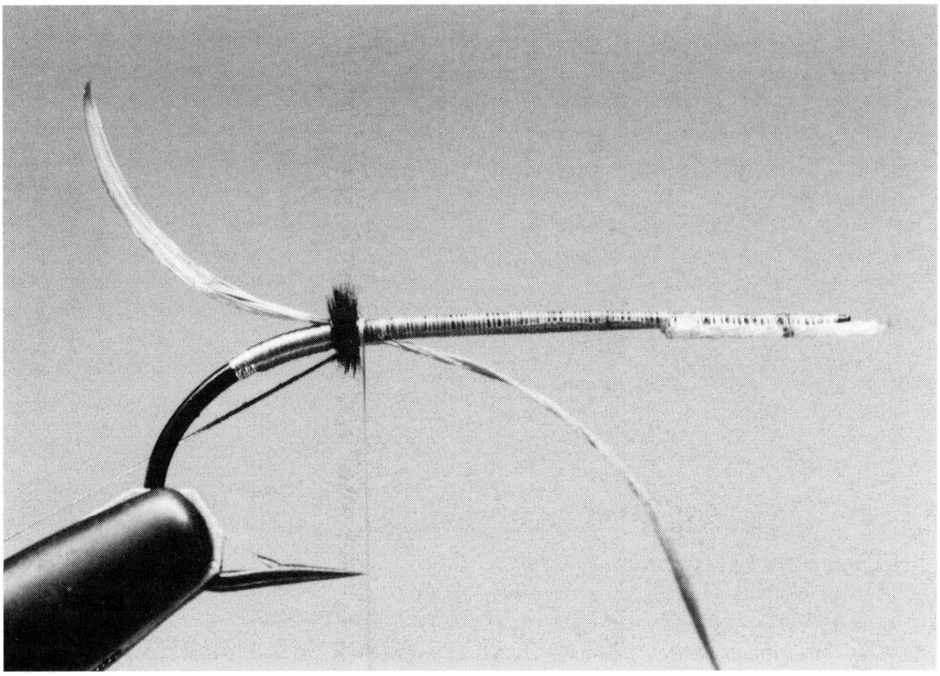

FIGURE 7-9

FIGURE 7-9

Strip enough metal off the core of the medium oval gold tinsel to have at least enough core to go from the tie-in point to the butt ends of the gut. Tie in the tinsel at five o'clock on the far side with one turn of thread, catching the least possible amount of metal. Make sure that some of the metal is under the thread, because when the tinsel is tied in at five o'clock and when it is later wound up the body, it comes out at six o'clock. If metal is not under the thread, the core will show.

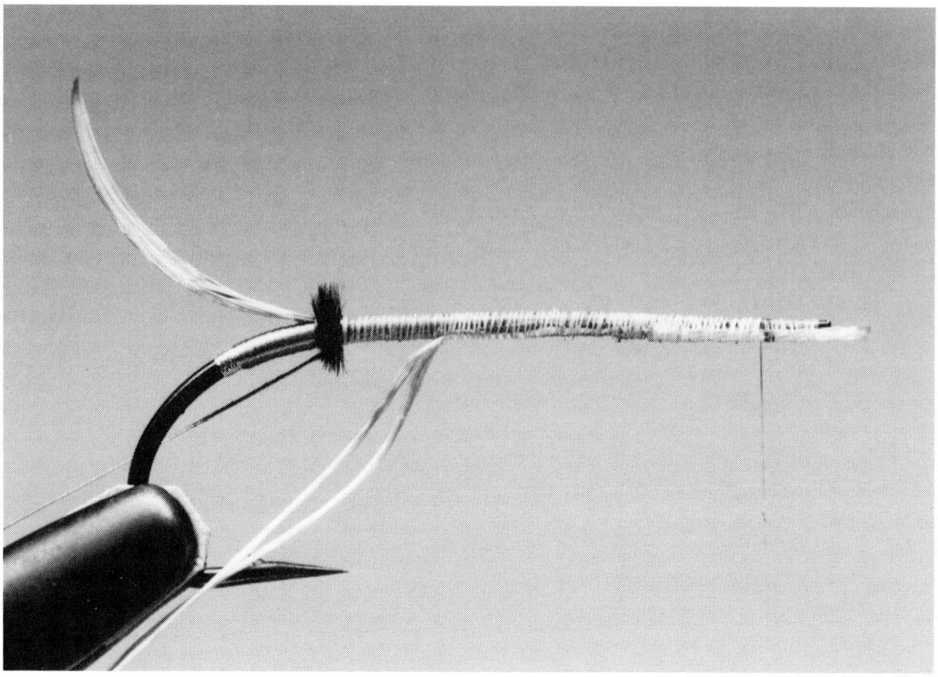

FIGURE 7-10

FIGURE 7-10
Wrap the thread forward, burying the core at six o'clock for about ¼ inch. With a ruler, measure ⅛ inch back from where the thread starts at the front end of the hook shank (do not include the $\frac{1}{32}$-inch tip of hook shank). Make a black mark on the thread. To judge how proportions are progressing, measure from in front of the butt to the black mark. For a standard 4/0 hook shank it should measure between 1 inch and $1\frac{1}{16}$ inches. A measurement shorter than that will make the body of the fly too short. $\frac{1}{16}$ inch longer or so is O.K.

Prepare two strands of white rayon floss 18 inches long and tie them in where the thread stops. Leave the waste ends a little longer than the hook shank. Wrapping forward, bury the tinsel core and floss together at six o'clock until they reach the butt end of the gut. The underbody has to be as smooth as possible. This may require the waste ends to be doubled back and forth, wrapped with thread, to smooth out the transition point where the waste ends meet the butt ends of the gut. Next, cut off the remaining short waste ends and wrap the thread forward to the black mark. Do not have any of the underbody or body parts go beyond the black ⅛-inch mark. That space is reserved for the throat, wings, and head.

I use rayon floss because of its effectiveness and ease in making underbodies. Hale recommended wool, while other early writers extended thick gut down the hook shank to just short of the point of the hook and shaved it to a taper. Rayon offers an easy solution provided by modern technology.

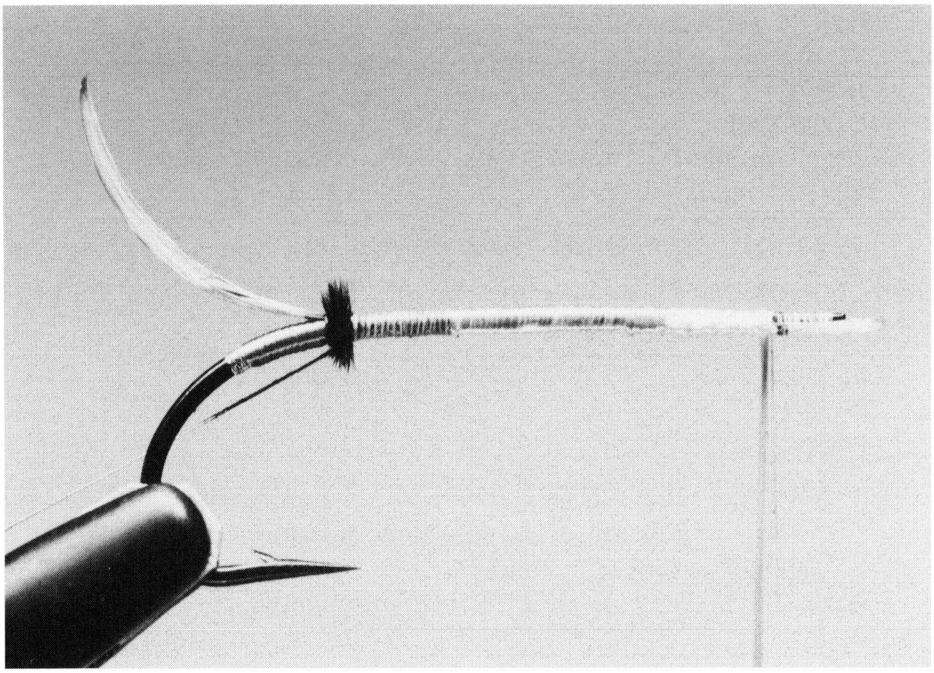

FIGURE 7-11

FIGURE 7-11
This photo shows the first layer of the two strands of rayon floss for the underbody after they have been wound forward, edge to edge. Note that there are no materials in front of the butt for the first ¼ inch except for two layers of thread.

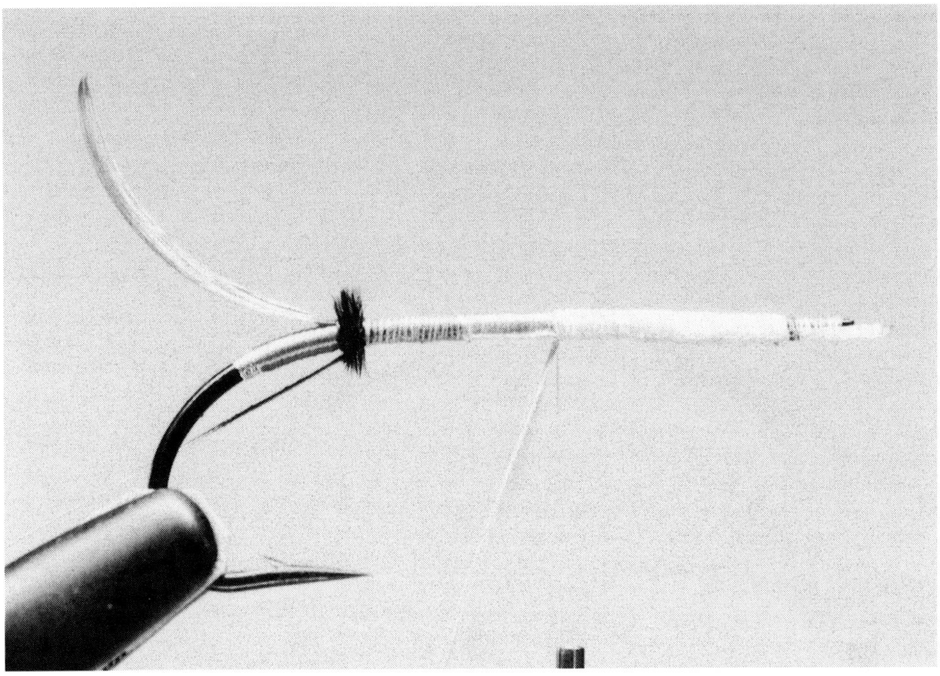

FIGURE 7-12

FIGURE 7-12
Wind the floss toward the rear of the body just slightly past the halfway point between the butt and the black mark. Hold the waste ends tightly with one hand and wrap the thread to where the floss stops with tight, close turns. Cut off the waste ends.

At the point where the floss was first tied in there will be a slight mound of floss. Take a few turns of thread to smooth it out, then follow through by wrapping the thread back to the front of the butt. The underbody now consists of ¼ inch of thread and ¼ inch of one layer of floss, in front of which are two layers of floss that cover the last half of the underbody.

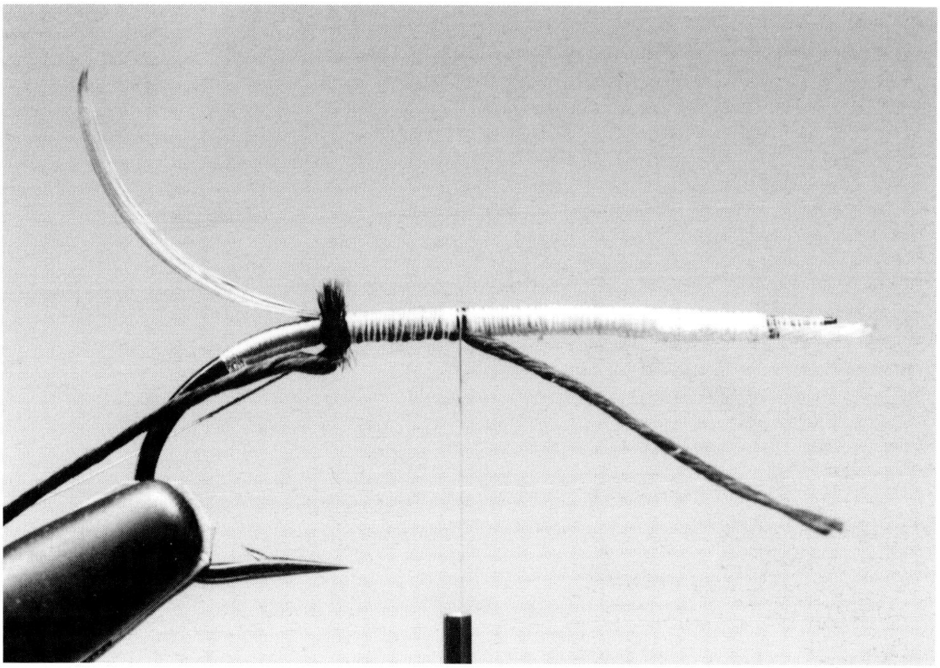

FIGURE 7-13

FIGURE 7-13

Measure ¼ inch from the front of the butt. Make a black mark.

Prepare the fly's body hackle by doubling a claret neck hackle. Always use neck hackles for bodies and saddle hackles or schlappen (preferred) for throats. A large number of flies are built with saddle hackles on the bodies. They do not have a gradual taper from the tie-in point to the throat because the barbs are nearly equal in length. Figure 7-14 shows the taper of neck hackle.

Tie in an 8-inch section of claret silk floss exactly in front of the butt. Wrap the thread forward to the ¼-inch mark. The waste end of silk floss will be used later to finely smooth the body if there is an indentation at six o'clock where the gut ends.

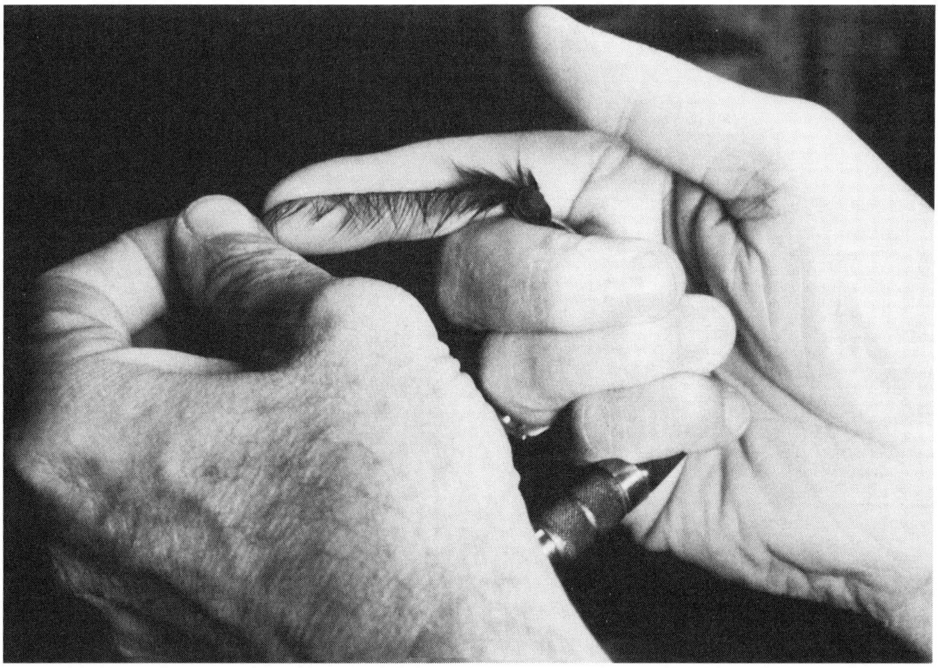

FIGURE 7-13A

FIGURE 7-13A

One technique used to double hackle is to hold the butt end of the hackle with hackle pliers as shown. Have the good (bright) side of the feather facing down, dull side up. With your other hand, hold the tip of the hackle with a lot of tension. Note the amount of pressure against your index finger. Without enough tension, the quill will roll. Moisten your thumb and index finger. Pinch the barbs together, then push them to the left and down. Work along the length of the feather until the tip is reached. This method of doubling hackle takes some practice, but the effect is worth the effort.

FIGURE 7-14

FIGURE 7-14

After wrapping the waste end of silk floss up to where the butts of gut are, wrap the thread back to the ¼-inch mark. Flatten the silk floss and wrap it forward, edge to edge, to the ¼-inch mark. Four or five wraps of floss will reach the ¼-inch black mark. Tie in the tip of the hackle with the last wrap of silk floss. The remaining tip of the hackle is then tied in with thread that is at the ¼-inch mark. Continue wrapping the thread forward and stop at the black ⅛-inch mark. Remember to hold the silk floss tight with one hand as the thread is wound forward. This is important: The tip of hackle must also be tied in with thread. It's a sure bet that when the hackle is wound forward it will pull out if the thread is not holding it.

FIGURE 7-15

FIGURE 7-15
Wrap the floss forward to the black mark. Tie it off at six o'clock with three turns of thread, one on top of the other.

Next, wrap the tinsel rib forward. The second turn is made in front of the hackle because the hackle is wound on behind the rib. Note from the instructions in chapter six that equal amounts of silk show at the beginning and end of the rib.

Do not cut off any waste ends yet. If a component pulls out or breaks, it is easier to unwrap and replace than it is to rebuild the whole body.

FIGURE 7-16

FIGURE 7-16

Wrap the hackle forward and behind each turn of ribbing. To make the effect of the hackle flowing toward the tail of the fly rather than standing up dry-fly fashion, push the hackle around the body with your index finger. Pulling it will make it stand up straight. Tie it off with three turns of thread one on top of the other at six o'clock.

Using tweezers, tear off the barbs one at a time that are on top of the body at twelve o'clock. These barbs would be in the way when setting wings and veilings. With your thumb and index finger, pinch the barbs together to enhance the effect of their flowing back toward the tail.

Cut off the waste ends and apply a drop of head cement.

FIGURE 7-17

FIGURE 7-17

Double a saddle or schlappen hackle. Hold it against the tie-in point just in front of the ⅛-inch black mark to judge which part of the hackle will be used to make the throat. For correct length, the barbs should be a bit longer than the body hackle, but not so long as to touch the point of the hook. A close look at the photo shows a 1/16-inch length of quill that has the barbs cut off. Tie that tip in halfway between the ⅛-inch mark and the end of the thread at six o'clock. Slip the thread in between the 1/32-inch tip of the hook and gut, then cut it off. Change over to black thread, size 6/0, and take three or four turns so that it holds itself.

FIGURE 7-18

FIGURE 7-18

Wind four turns of the throat hackle on as a collar. Make sure all wraps are in front of the ⅛-inch black mark. Tie the hackle off with three or four turns of thread. Cut off the waste end of the hackle that remains after taking four turns. If the turns of hackle with its quill end up on the tip of the hook shank or on the gut eye, it will not be a problem because the turns of quill will be cut off, as shown in figure 7-20.

FIGURE 7-19

FIGURE 7-19

Separate the barbs at twelve o'clock and pull them down and back. The black ⅛-inch mark should be visible. Tie off the throat with four or five turns of thread, each on top of the last, exactly on top of the mark. Apply a heavy drop of head cement and let it dry for a couple of minutes.

FIGURE 7-20

FIGURE 7-20

Hale recommends cutting off the quill on thick-quilled feathers such as guinea fowl to reduce unwanted bulk. The same procedure applied to all flies reduces bulk and contributes significantly to heads that will be in proportion to the size of the fly being built.

Using a razor blade held at a 45-degree angle to the hook shank, cut through the barbs in front of the thread and remove the coils of quill. Be careful not to cut the gut. If the thread is accidentally cut, the head cement will hold it in place until it can be resecured. Sometimes I use scissors to cut the quill off after cutting through the barbs with a razor blade.

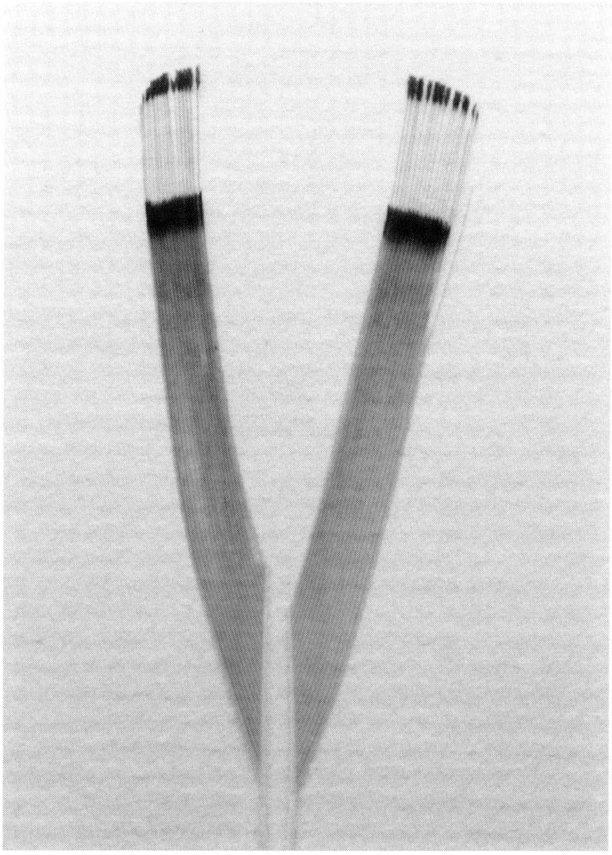

FIGURE 7-21

FIGURE 7-21

Select a right and left golden pheasant tippet from the longest on a neck. Prepare them by having their good (bright) sides up and stripping off the inside barbs. Inside barbs will be the shortest barbs on each feather. Do not split the quills. Strip off the downy short barbs on the outside of the feathers at the butt ends. Cut off the other ends, leaving strips about ¼ inch wide with the quill intact. This is a difficult step to describe in words. Study the photo, and prepare a left and right tippet to look like the ones shown. The good (bright) sides of the feathers are up in the photograph.

FIGURE 7-22

FIGURE 7-22

Place the strips back to back, dull sides on the inside facing each other. Position them above the hook so the two black stripes on the tippets straddle the butt. Holding the strips between your left thumb and index finger, take the thread up on the near side, over the top, down the far side, and back up the near side. Apply pressure on the thread and strips with your thumb and index finger. Pull straight up. The objective is to stack the barbs, one on top of the other at twelve o'clock. Often the strips will roll. When that happens, release the thread pressure and try again. It may require two or more attempts before the strips sit properly. Another problem that may occur is that the last turn of ribbing may have a tendency to push the strips up. A solution is to put a drop of head cement on the shoulder of the strips just left of the tie-in point and hold them while the cement dries.

After the strips are in their proper place, put a drop of head cement on the thread.

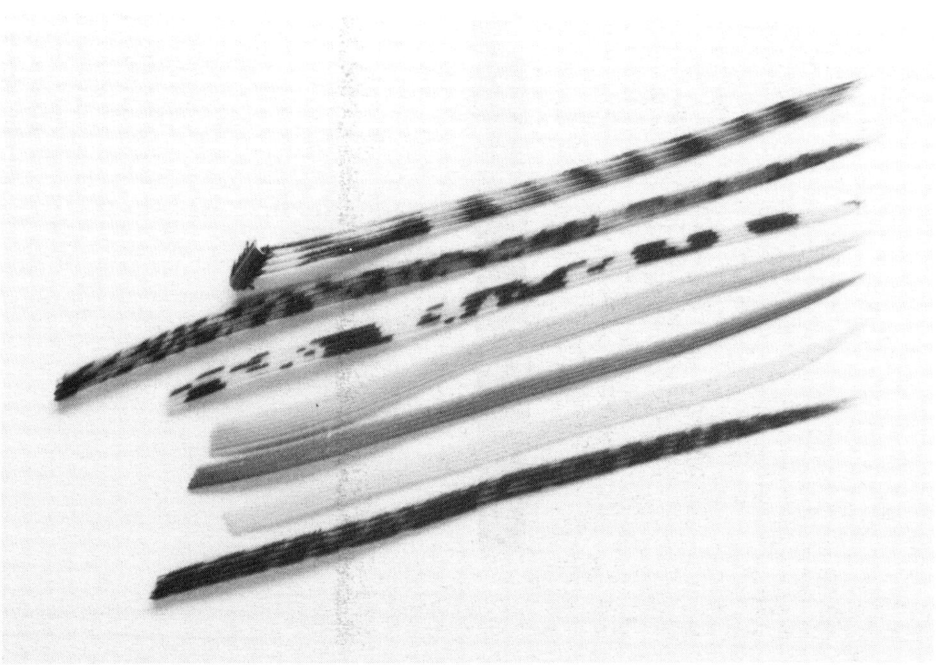

FIGURE 7-23

FIGURE 7-23

Note: With the fly in the vise, the head is on the right and the tail is on the left. The wing facing the tyer is the left wing/near side. The wing on the opposite side is the right wing/far side.

It is very easy to confuse left and right wing strips. When that happens and there is no one to point out the error, frustration sets in quickly. A left strip can be married to a right strip, but right strips that follow will not marry the left strip. So, the best recourse is to build one wing at a time.

Start with the right wing, which is for the far side of the fly. Have the bright side of the feathers facing you. Cut strips approximately $\frac{1}{8}$ inch wide from the right side of each type of feather used in the wing. Position them in the order in which they are to be married, from the bottom of the wing to the top, with their dull sides facing up. Note where the cut ends are, as opposed to the tips of the strips. For the golden pheasant tail, leave the quill attached. Marry the strips by pushing their edges together so that the natural hooks on the barbs will interlock with each other. Have the tips of the strips even, and when marrying them, have the bright side facing down. The dull side faces up. In other words, looking at the dull sides, the strips are concave.

Marry the strips from the bottom to the top: first dark turkey; then yellow, blue, and red goose (alternatives for swan); peacock wing; mottled turkey (alternative for speckled bustard); finish with golden pheasant tail.

FIGURE 7-24

FIGURE 7-24
This is a repeat of the steps used in making the right wing for the far side, except that the strips are cut from the left side of each type of feather used in the wing. Note where the cut ends are in the left wing, which is for the near side of the fly. This left wing is married with the good (bright) sides facing up, and the dull sides are down. It is the exact opposite of the right wing; looking at them, the good (bright) side of the strips are convex.

FIGURE 7-25

FIGURE 7-25

Both wings are shown here with their good (bright) sides facing up. The top wing is for the right/far side. At the bottom is the left/near-side wing. To ensure that the wings are built correctly, lay them next to those in the photo and compare the angles of the cut ends and the order in which the strips are married.

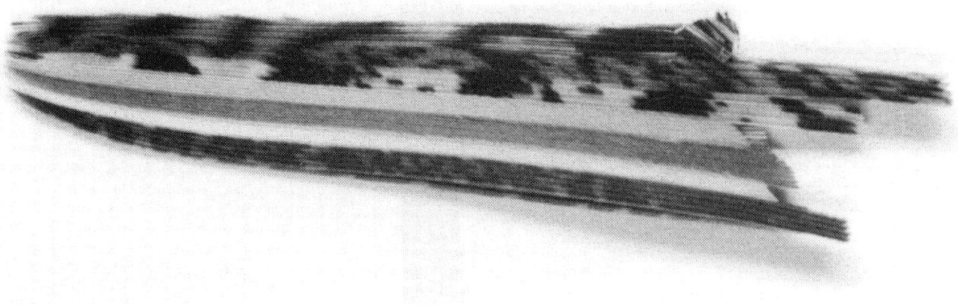

FIGURE 7-26

FIGURE 7-26
Wings are shown back to back, dull sides on the inside.

FIGURE 7-27

FIGURE 7-27

Set the wings on to straddle the golden pheasant tippet underwings. Make sure the tips of both wings are even at their ends and are just touching the tip of the tail. The procedures for tying in the wings are the same as explained in figure 7-22. Rarely do they set properly on the first attempt. When the strips collapse on themselves as shown in this photo, release the thread pressure and try again. A word of caution: After repeated attempts to set the wings, the strips can become so mangled that they cannot be stacked. When that happens, it is better to start over with a new pair.

FIGURE 7-28

FIGURE 7-28

If thread pressure has to be relaxed for a second or third attempt to set the wings, there will be a crease where the thread was wrapped and the strips were compressed. Realigning the strips and setting the wings will be easier because the wing is now halfway compressed. Half the wing height will not have to be controlled. This procedure can be referred to as *fitting the wing in place,* because the wing strips are partially compressed. Although it is not ideal, a slight overlapping of strips is acceptable because the wing veiling will cover them. The distinctive feature to try to establish is a pronounced hump at the shoulder of the wing. A good move now is to check where the turns of thread are lying. Each turn should be on top of the preceding wrap, and they should cover the ⅛-inch mark. Remember, too, use only enough turns to hold materials in place. Four tight turns should be enough to hold the wings.

Finally, put a full drop of head cement on the thread.

From this step until the last, as components are tied in, apply head cement.

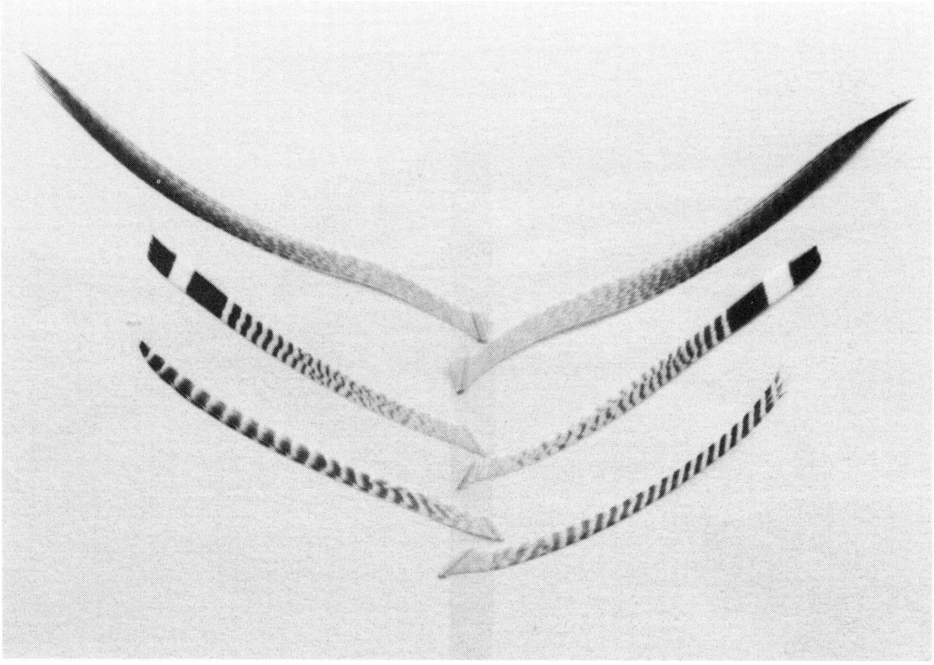

FIGURE 7-29

FIGURE 7-29
Wing Veilings and Roofing. From bottom to top: teal (for which pintail is a common alternative), barred wood duck, and bronze mallard (for roofing). As with the wing strips, the left sides of the feathers go on the left side of the wing (the near side). Right strips are for the far side. With all waterfowl feathers, leave the quill on the strips, as they are not as sturdy as tail and shoulder feathers. The quill helps to hold them together until they are tied in. The width of each strip should equal the width of one wing strip.

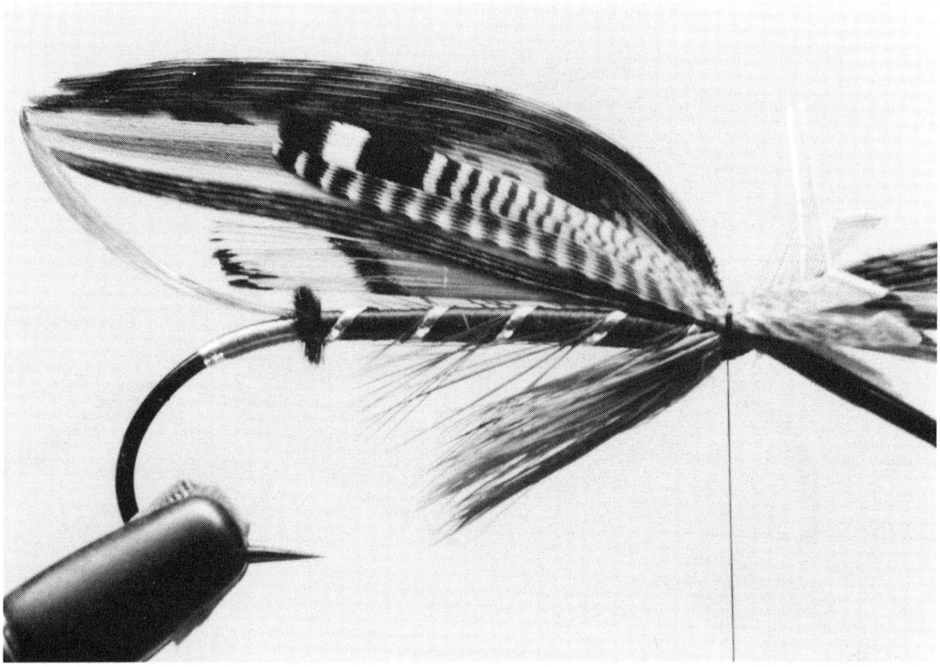

FIGURE 7-30

FIGURE 7-30
Marry the strips with the teal on the bottom. The components should be of a length that leaves enough room for the guinea fowl and kingfisher to be seen and does not cover the three bars of wood duck (see plate 13).

With normal wings, thread pressure on the near side causes the strips to push up and out. On the far side, pressure pulls the strips in as if they were glued because the thread pressure is pushing down and in. The way to avoid this problem is to position the strips and then, holding them in place with thumb and index finger, make a half turn with a loose loop of thread over the tie-in point; then let the bobbin drop. The weight of the bobbin will equalize the pressure on both sides. Take two more normal turns and finish this step with a drop of head cement.

FIGURE 7-31

FIGURE 7-31

Applying bronze mallard strips so that they lie on top of the wing at twelve o'clock can be difficult unless a specific technique is used. The key is to have the two strips marry from the tie-in point to their tips. Hold the strips above the tie-in point so their edges come together when thread pressure is applied. If they are low on the side of the wing, the front edges will not marry. In the photo, note their height as they sit on top of the tie-in point. Also notice that when they are married at the tie-in point, the rear ⅔ may have a tendency to ride high on the wings. Occasionally the roofing will not follow the contour of the wing. When this happens, put three or four tiny drops of liquid wax on the top edge of the wings, then push the strips in place. Be cautious with the amount of wax used. Too much can make a mess of everything, particularly if the wax bleeds through the feathers. Wax and fingertips should never come in contact with each other. Touching any part of the fly with residual wax on your fingers will pull it apart. If wax is needed, it's always best to apply it after the fly has been completed.

If the bronze mallard insists on working its way down the sides of the wing just behind the tie-in point, it may be necessary to pull the strips up toward each other until their edges come together and marry. Sometimes just one strip will need coaxing into place.

FIGURE 7-32

FIGURE 7-32
When the horns are tied in they will help the bronze mallard strips lie flat against the wings.

FIGURE 7-33

FIGURE 7-33

For the guinea fowl wing veiling, strips from a pair of primary wing quills work well because of their substantial barb density (as compared with saddle or flank feathers). Tie the strips in so their tips just meet the first bar of the barred wood duck. Don't forget the drop of head cement.

FIGURE 7-34

FIGURE 7-34

After the head cement dries a little, cut off the waste ends at a 45-degree angle. A razor blade works well for making a clean cut. Scissors can disrupt the set of the wings unless the head cement is completely dry.

The most important part of a salmon fly, and the one that has more effect than any other on the overall appearance, is the golden pheasant crest. Be very choosy when selecting it. Look for vivid color, brilliance, and curvature that will follow the contour of the wings to the extent that the tip will curve down to meet the tip of the tail. Occasionally crests have quills that are thicker than the norm. Even with steaming, they will not curve enough to meet the above criterion.

FIGURE 7-35

FIGURE 7-35
After steaming, hold the crest on the fly as it is in figure 7-34 and estimate where the tie-in point will be. With tweezers make a crimp there.

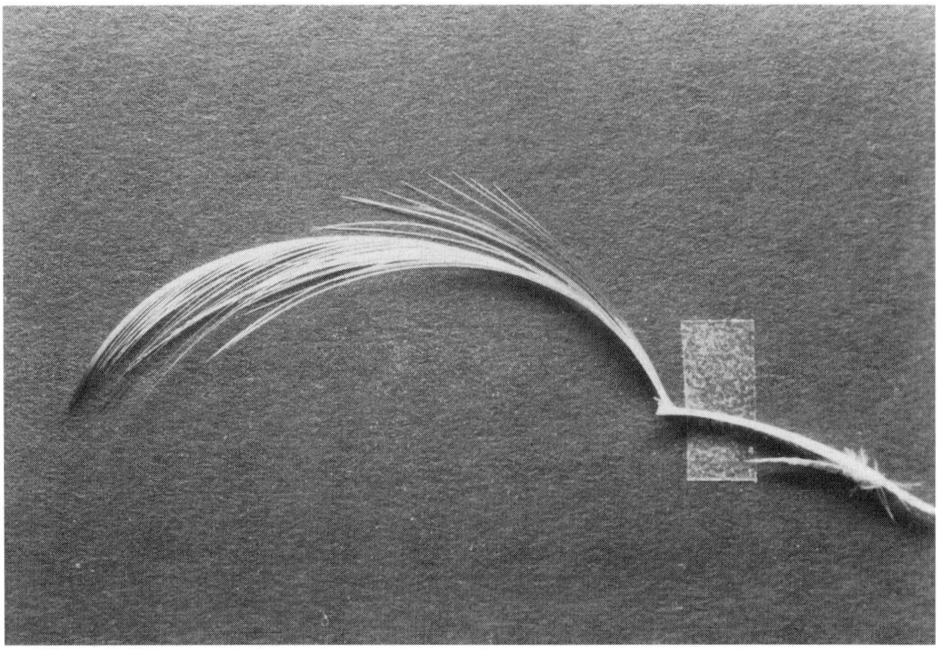

FIGURE 7-36

FIGURE 7-36
This is Hale's method for fitting the crest to the fly. Bend the quill with tweezers to curve along the top edge of the shoulder of the wing and then strip off the barbs that are forced up from bending the quill.

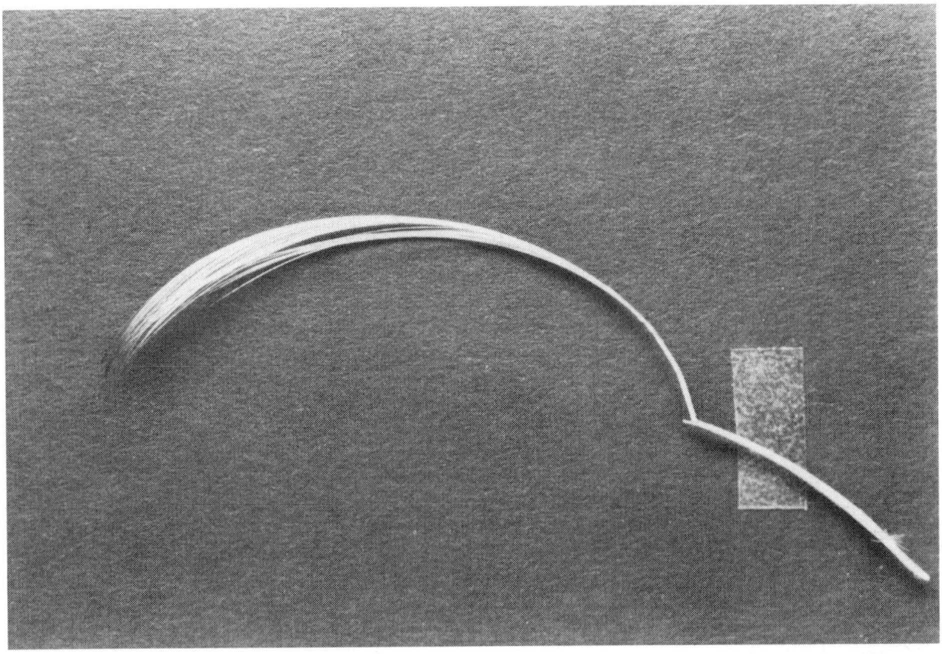

FIGURE 7-37

FIGURE 7-37

The crest is now ready to be tied on. Notice the bend in the butt end of the crest and how it duplicates the natural curve at the tip of the crest. This will give a nice look of balance to the fly. Remember to steam the crest. The slightest twist in the quill makes it difficult for the crest to follow along the top of the wing.

FIGURE 7-38

FIGURE 7-38

If the crest is too long or too short and does not meet the tip of the tail, it may have to be crimped again.

FIGURE 7-39

FIGURE 7-39

Select and tie in the kingfisher saddle hackle by catching a couple of the barbs so the feather doesn't roll. Note that the wing veilings are proportioned so that each can be seen.

FIGURE 7-40

FIGURE 7-40

The blue-and-yellow macaw horns, left and right, are the last components to be tied in. Looking at the cut end of an individual barb, it is T-shaped. The barb is blue on top and yellow on each side. Tie each barb in with the yellow flat against the side of the head and the blue up. This will prevent any rolling of the barbs.

FIGURE 7-41

FIGURE 7-41

Cut off the waste ends of the crest and horns, one at a time. It is a good idea to hold the wing while cutting off the crest. The head cement is not completely dry, and pressure from scissors can easily move the crest out of alignment. Wrap and form a round and bullet-shaped head with thread. Apply three or more coats of head cement or black Cellire varnish, allowing ample drying time between coats. Cellire makes a very nice head. In high humidity, clear lacquer head cement will dry cloudy.

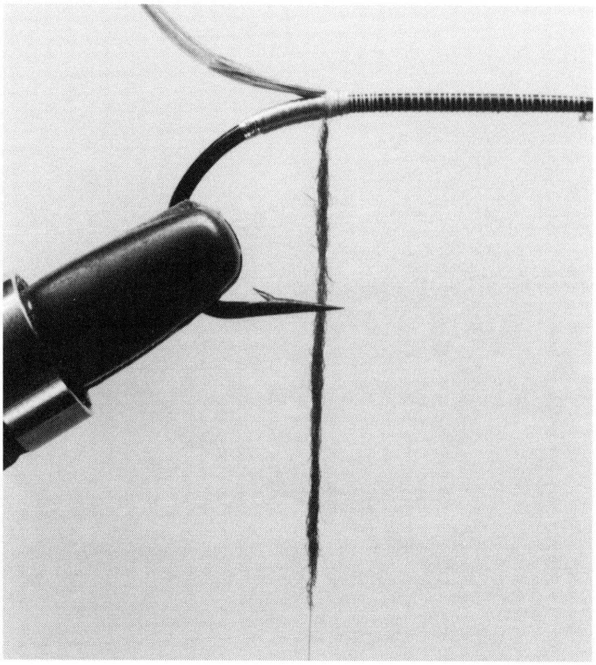

FIGURE 7-42

Silver Doctor (plate 14)

This section covers dressing a fly with a wool butt, a flat-tinsel body, and a wool head.

The beginning of the fly is covered in figures 7-1 through 7-6.

FIGURE 7-42

On a single strand of prewaxed thread, twist on the prepared scarlet wool, using only enough to color the thread. In this photo, the "rope of fur" is magnified. In reality, it has to be very thin to reduce bulk. (See chapter two for information on wool preparation.)

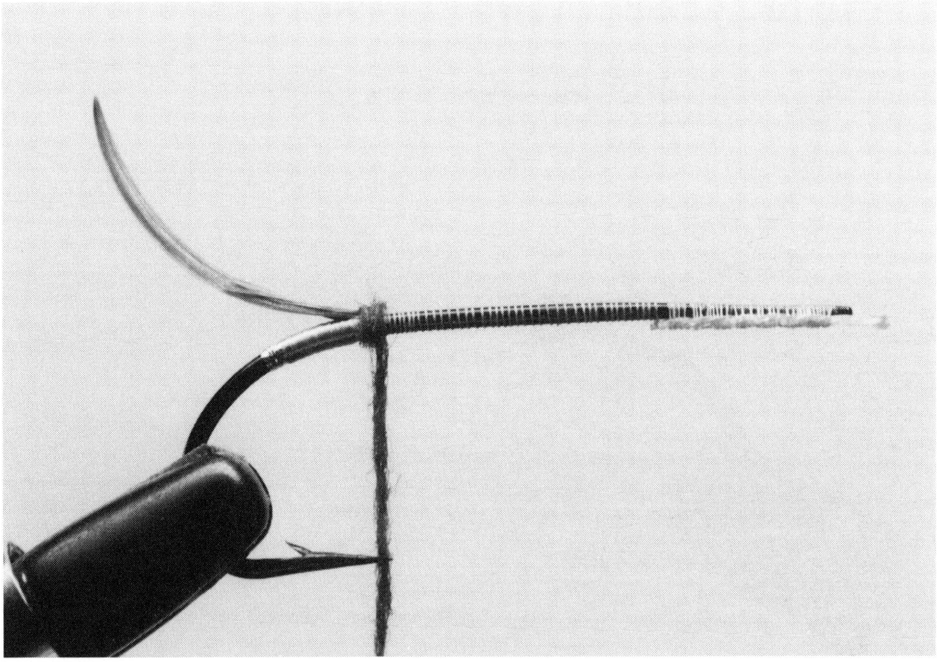

FIGURE 7-43

FIGURE 7-43
Hale's instructions call for a wool butt, oval in shape. To form an oval shape, take one wrap left, one wrap right, followed by two wraps in the center, one on top of the other.

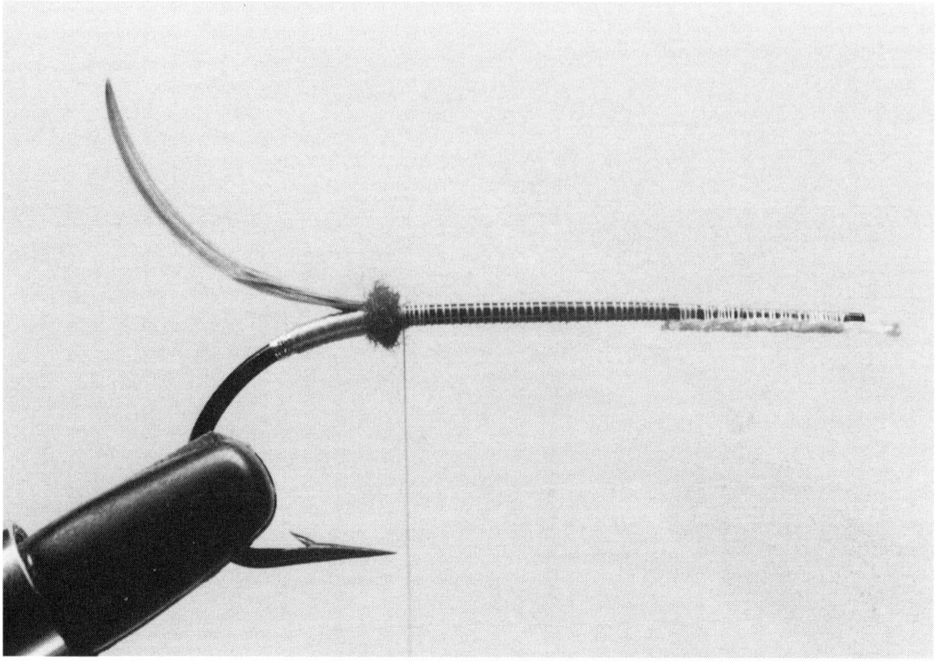

FIGURE 7-44

FIGURE 7-44
If any wool remains on the fur rope below the last wrap, pull it off and secure the butt with one turn of thread.

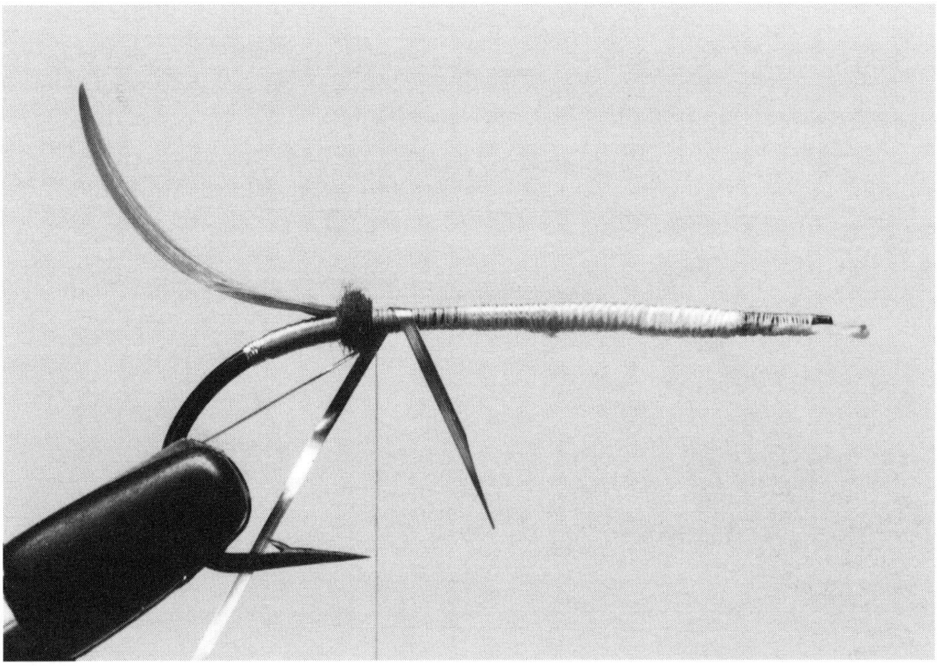

FIGURE 7-45

FIGURE 7-45

Prepare the fine oval tinsel rib and build the underbody as shown in figures 7-9 through 7-12. However, have the black mark 3⁄16 inch from the end of the shank to leave room for the wool head. In this photo, the flat tinsel for the body is draped over the body to show how it is cut at an angle. Tie in just the tip of the cut section at five o'clock on the far side with the cut edge facing forward. Wrap the thread forward to the black mark. Take close turns of thread to smooth out the body. Another word of caution: As the tip of the tinsel is wrapped in, be careful that the thread is not wound too tightly. The sharp edge of the tinsel can easily cut it.

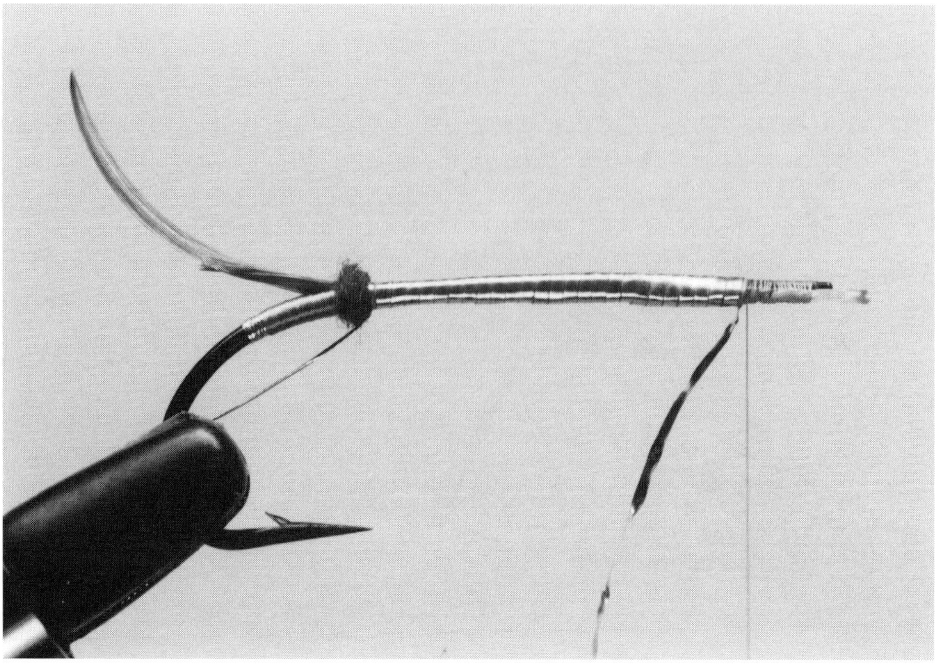

FIGURE 7-46

FIGURE 7-46

Pryce-Tannatt was very specific in his instructions for building a flat-tinsel body: "Each turn of the flat tinsel must fit close up to the preceding turn, *but not under any circumstances must there be any overlapping*." Without a tapered body, the tinsel will not wrap with each turn tight against the preceding edge. After wrapping the tinsel forward, tie it off with three turns of thread, remembering that the sharp edge can still cut thread.

FIGURE 7-47

FIGURE 7-47

Wrap the oval tinsel forward with the traditional five turns for ribs. Tie it off at six o'clock. Cut off the tinsel waste ends. Apply a drop of head cement. Sometimes the core of the oval tinsel will stretch, and with the slippery surface of the flat tinsel, the ribs may come loose and slide down the tapered body. To prevent this, a touch of head cement on the third turn of ribbing on the far side will help keep it in place.

FIGURE 7-48

FIGURE 7-48
Except for the double throat, which has two or three turns of each type of feather (depending on their thickness), and strips of golden pheasant tail over the underwing, the fly is built as shown in figures 7-21 through 7-39. Some steps are eliminated because some components are not in the dressing for the Silver Doctor.

The two side feathers adjacent to the center tail feathers of golden pheasant are much easier to work with regardless of whether they are used in wings or underwings. Leave the quill on the strips. Underwings should be ¼ inch, or slightly less, in width. Tie them in using the same technique explained in figure 7-22. Have the right strip of feather on the left side of the underwing and the left side on the right. With this method they will have a natural curve down over the tippet underwing. Use three snug turns of thread and apply a full drop of head cement. Do not cut off any waste ends yet. The waste ends of tippet and golden pheasant tail make an excellent foundation to help support the wings when they are tied in.

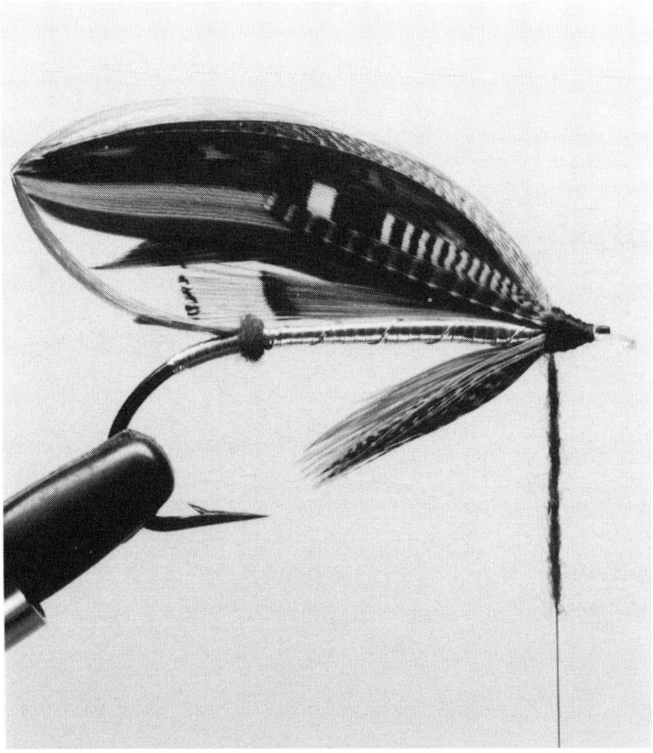

FIGURE 7-49

FIGURE 7-49
Make a rope of red wool, again with only enough wool to color the thread. Have it long enough to make at least two wraps around the head. Three wraps may be too much.

FIGURE 7-50

FIGURE 7-50
Whip finish the head and put on a coating of head cement. It's good to let a little of the head cement bleed up into the wool. It holds the wool in place, and after it dries, the wool returns to its natural color. Complete the fly with three coats of Cellire varnish or head cement.

A judgment call in this dressing is the length of the wing veiling. As it consists only of teal and wood duck, it does not have to be as long as on the Parson in figure 7-31.

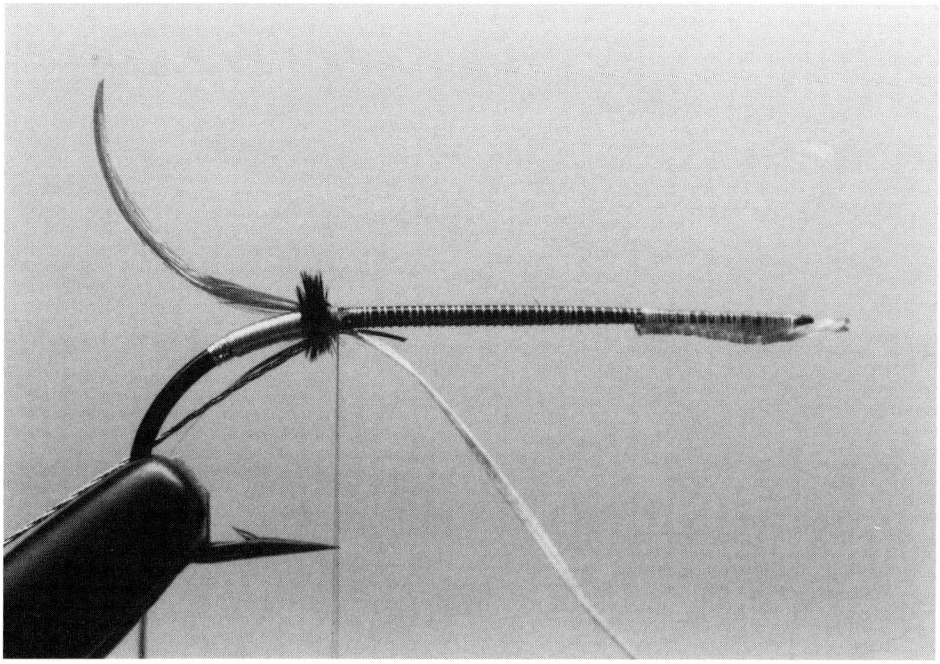

FIGURE 7-51

Durham Ranger (plate 6)

FIGURE 7-51

Complete the first part of the fly as shown in figures 7-1 through 7-8. Tie off the herl butt with one turn of thread. The pattern calls for fine silver lace and narrow silver flat tinsel for ribs. Strip off 2 inches of metal from the lace and tie it in at five o'clock on the far side. Remember to catch a bit of the metal under the thread. Tie in the flat tinsel on top of the lace, again at five o'clock. A quarter inch of waste is enough to secure it. The first rib to be wound forward is the last rib tied in.

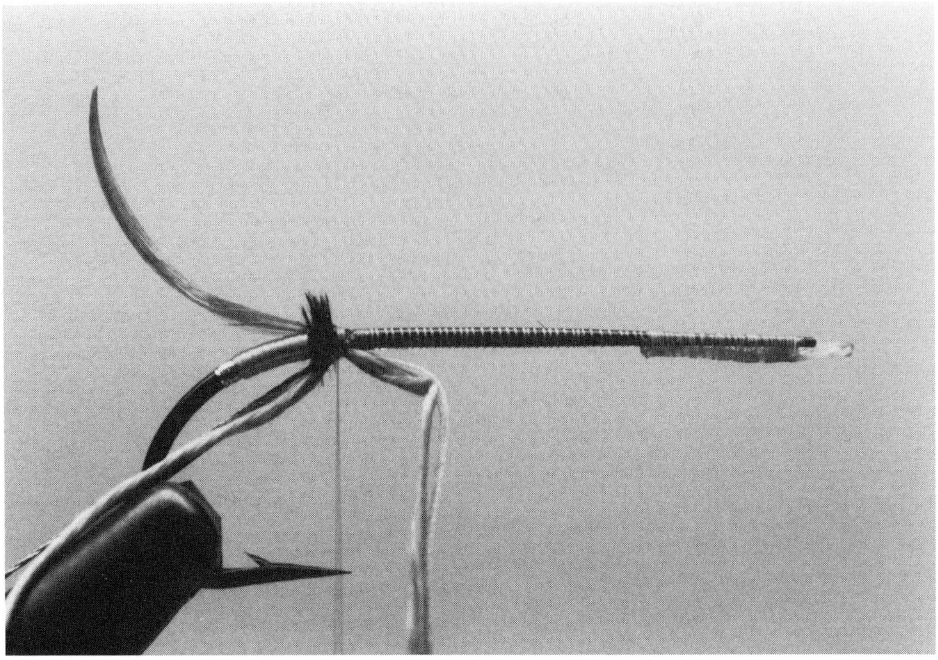

FIGURE 7-52

FIGURE 7-52

Tie in a 4-inch piece of silk floss at six o'clock. The waste ends of floss and lace core are wrapped in at six o'clock up to the waste ends of the gut.

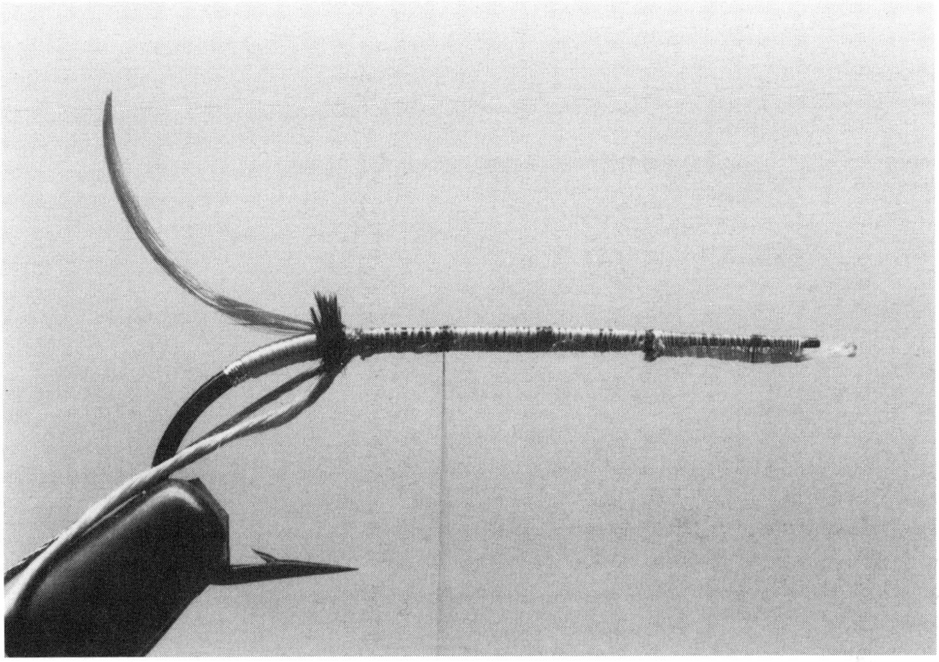

FIGURE 7-53

FIGURE 7-53

Because ¾ of the body is seal's fur, this pattern will not require an underbody. When the butt end of the gut is reached, cut off any remaining waste ends of floss and tinsel core. Wrap the thread back to ¼ inch in front of the butt. Make the ⅛-inch mark (see figure 7-10), then divide the length of the hook shank between the butt and front mark into four equal sections. Each section on a 4/0 hook will be about ¼ inch wide. Twist the floss one way or the other to flatten it. Wrap it forward to the first ¼-inch mark, overlapping a little of the floss with each turn around the hook shank. Easy does it; do not overlap the floss too much—just enough to make a slight forward taper. Tie off the silk floss at the first ¼-inch mark with three turns of thread. Cut off the waste end of silk floss at six o'clock.

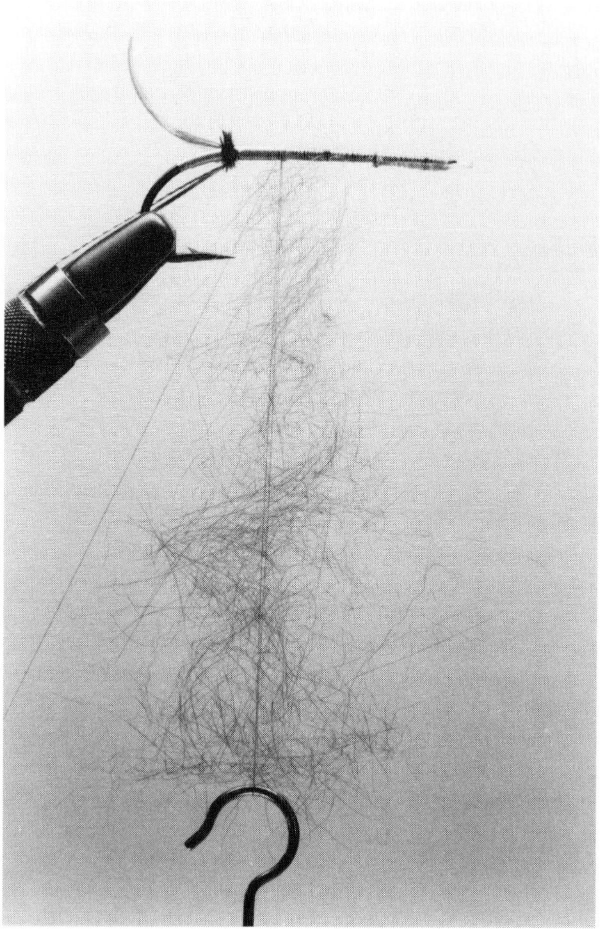

FIGURE 7-54

FIGURE 7-54
After tying off the silk floss, make a 4-inch loop of thread by bringing the thread down to and then over the left index finger, then back up to the point where the floss is tied off at the first ¼-inch mark. Go over the top of the hook shank, then bring the bobbin back under the hook shank and take two turns of thread around the two sections of thread to form a loop. Have the two turns of thread tight up against the bottom of the hook shank at six o'clock.

Hold the loop open with the index finger, then put thin pinches of orange seal's fur in the loop. Try to have the staple of the fur on a horizontal plane. If the fur insists on falling out of the loop, wipe the bottom thread with liquid wax. That will hold the fur in place until the loop is filled with fur and the shepherd's hook replaces your index finger. Study the photo to see how the fur is distributed in equal amounts, and that the staple is longer at the bottom of the loop than at the top. By increasing the width of the fur toward the bottom of the loop, you increase the quantity of the fur that is twisted with the shepherd's hook to make a fur rope. In turn, as the fur rope is wound on the shank, it helps give a taper to the body because of the larger amount of fur that is being wound in.

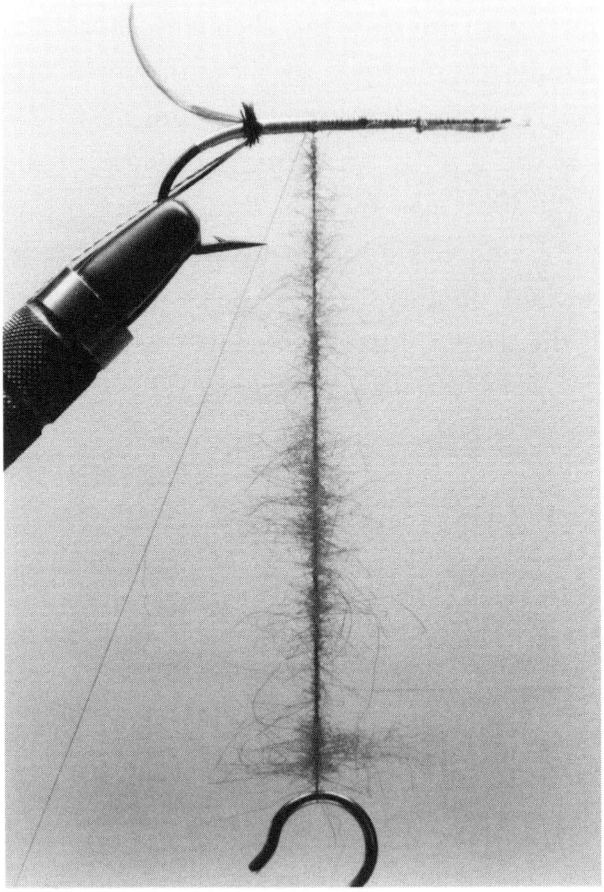

FIGURE 7-55

FIGURE 7-55

In figures 7-54 and 7-55 the bobbin and thread were held to the left so they would not obstruct the view of the loop. Twist the loop clockwise with the shepherd's hook until the thread disappears into the fur rope. In this first section of seal's fur only, and for 1 inch of the rope from the bottom of the hook shank down the rope, trim off any long staples of fur.

FIGURE 7-56

FIGURE 7-56

Double the hackle as shown in figure 7-13A. Position the tip of the hackle between the fur rope and the thread underneath the hook shank at six o'clock. Wrap the thread forward to the second ¼-inch mark. The hackle can be tied in before building the fur rope; however, it will be easier to tie it in after the rope is made. Whichever method is used, it is imperative that the tip of the hackle be secured with thread. Odds are 20 to 1 that if it is anchored only with the fur rope, it will pull out when it is wrapped forward. Wrap the orange fur forward to the thread at the second ¼-inch mark.

Before taking each wrap forward, use your left thumb and index finger to pull the fur that is on top of the shank down and back. The object is to have as much fur as possible under the hook shank in comparison to the amount that remains on top. When you reach the second mark, there should be a small amount of waste rope remaining. Untwist the rope to open the short section of the loop. Reach up and pull the loose fur down from the tie-in point. Tie off the loop with three tight wraps of thread. Cut off the waste ends of the loop.

Make the second loop for the fiery brown fur by repeating the procedures in figures 7-54 through 7-56, except for tapering the fur (figure 7-54). The width of the staple of the fiery brown fur and the black fur should be equal.

Make the third loop for the black fur and repeat each of the preceding steps.

FIGURE 7-57

FIGURE 7-57

Don't despair—it isn't as bad as it looks. After the fur is formed as shown in figure 7-58, the outline of the body will appear as though the fur had been picked out. Notice that there is a lot of fur under the hook shank and hardly any on top.

FIGURE 7-58

FIGURE 7-58

To form the body, first take six extra turns of thread at the tie-off point to prevent the body from coming apart when the fur is picked off. With your thumb and index finger, pick off as much fur as possible from the top of the body; then use tweezers to pick off the rest. The top of the body has to be as smooth as possible. Do *not* trim it with scissors. Breaking the staple off will make it look natural. The fur under the body can also be shaped if necessary.

FIGURE 7-59

FIGURE 7-59
Unwrap the six extra turns of thread that were used to keep the body from coming apart while the fur was picked off. Next, wrap the flat tinsel forward. It's a good idea to separate the fur with the point of a shepherd's hook to make room for the tinsel. After all the trouble of pulling down and back each wrap of fur to make it look as if it had been picked out, why pack it down with tinsel? Tie off the flat tinsel at six o'clock. Twist the lace tinsel together tightly in case it had separated at the tie-in point in front of the butt. The lace goes directly behind the flat tinsel. Tie off both types of tinsel with three turns of thread. Next, bring the hackle forward in back of the lace. Tie it off at six o'clock. Barbs of the hackle will be protruding above the body at twelve o'clock. Pick them off one at a time with tweezers. When everything looks good, apply a heavy drop of head cement at the tie-off points and cut off the waste ends.

FIGURE 7-60

FIGURE 7-60
Using a light blue schlappen hackle, repeat the steps for the throat as detailed in figures 7-17 through 7-20.

Select two large feathers of jungle cock for the underwing. Determine the tie-in point, then strip off the barbs that would lie on top of the tinsel ribs. Notice in the photo how the barbs that would have come in contact with the ribs have been stripped off. If the barbs are left on the quills, the ribs will force the underwing high, and the tips of jungle cock will not touch the tip of the tail.

Apply a drop of head cement at the tie-in point. Do not cut off the waste ends of the jungle cock. Leave them for now as a foundation for the tippets.

FIGURE 7-61

FIGURE 7-61

In selecting golden pheasant tippets for the wing, it is most important to choose the correct size to fit the hook. To create overall good proportions, they cannot be too long or sit too high on the body. Remembering that the objective is to have the tip of the crest touch the tip of the tail, you must choose the tippets carefully. The rule of thumb is to have the first pair tied in no wider at their first black bar than the gap of the hook. If a large pair of tippets is chosen, and half of the barbs are stripped off to make the feather short enough to fill in the length of the body, it will still be too wide at the ends and sit too high. The golden pheasant crest will not come down to touch the tail.

Pull a tippet away from the neck and hold it on the gap of the hook. If it matches the gap and is long enough to fill the length of the body, match it with a left or right tippet—whichever is needed. A pair of tippets can also be tied in upside-down. Observe the black bars of the feather in the photo. If this pair were rotated 180 degrees and tied in, they would be too high, and the crest would not meet the tail.

Strip off the downy barbs at the base of the feathers. Straddle the tippets over the jungle cock underwing and tie them in with three very tight turns of thread. It requires a lot of thread pressure to hold them in place.

Select the shorter pair of tippets and tie them in with their quills to the left and right of the quills of the first pair. Have the first black bar of the second pair lying on top of the second bar on the first pair. Apply a full drop of head cement at the tie-in point.

In the photo the tippets appear to be a little wider than the height of the hook gap. When the crest is tied in as demonstrated in figure 7-64, it compresses the tippets to an exact fit equal to the gap of the hook.

FIGURE 7-62

FIGURE 7-62
Length and size of the jungle cock wing veilings is a judgment call. Their length gives a trim look to the fly, and the size of the eyes should be smaller than those in the underwing.

FIGURE 7-63

FIGURE 7-63

Tie in the kingfisher cheeks. Because their blue color doesn't come through that well in black and white, you may have to examine the photo more closely to see how they are positioned.

FIGURE 7-64

FIGURE 7-64

Fashion the crest as it is in figures 7-35 through 7-37. Tie it in directly on top of the wing edge at twelve o'clock.

FIGURE 7-65

FIGURE 7-65
Secure the macaw horns as explained in figure 7-40.

FIGURE 7-66

FIGURE 7-66

Cut off the waste ends. Wrap and form a bullet-shaped head with the thread and whip finish. Apply a coat of head cement, and then finish with three or four coats of head cement or black Cellire varnish.

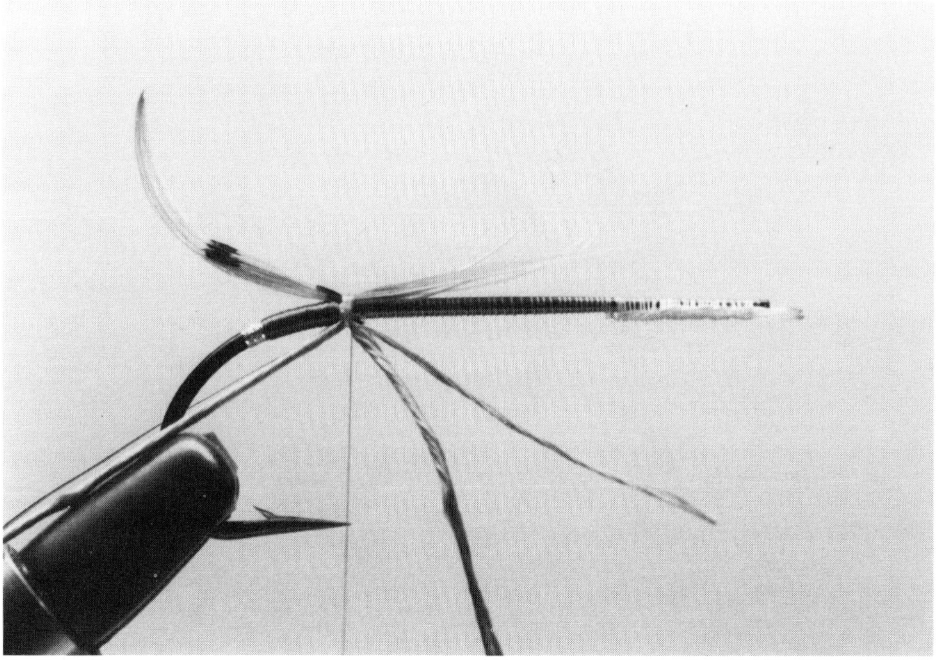

FIGURE 7-67

Orange Parson (plate 12)

The Orange Parson and a few other patterns are built without butts. In these patterns, the waste ends of the tail and tail veiling are not cut off, but instead are buried on top of the hook shank at twelve o'clock to form a smooth body.

FIGURE 7-67
Complete the first part of the fly as shown in figures 7-1 through 7-6. Tie in the medium oval gold tinsel at five o'clock on the far side. Tie in the orange silk floss at six o'clock. Have the waste ends of the tinsel core and floss long enough to reach the butt ends of the gut.

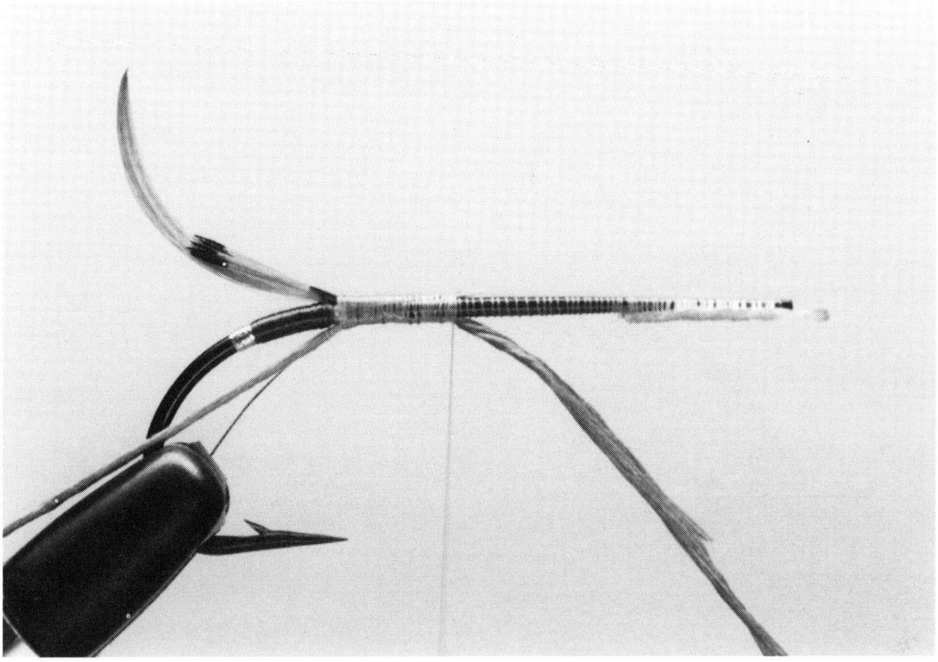

FIGURE 7-68

FIGURE 7-68

Wrap the thread forward, burying the waste ends of the tail and tail veiling. Any remaining waste ends of the tail are now cut off after the first section of the orange floss is wrapped in.

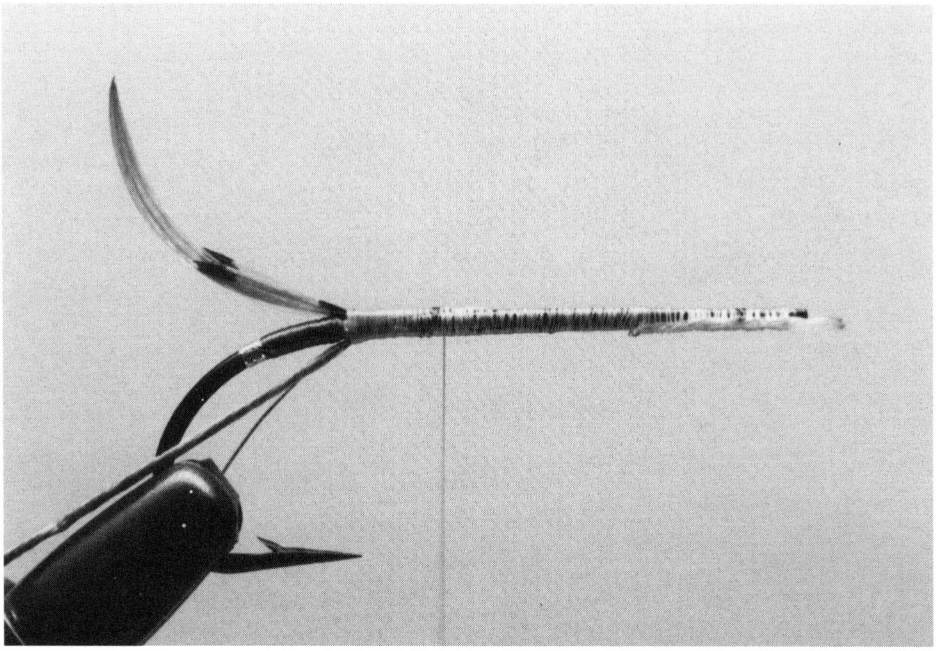

FIGURE 7-69

FIGURE 7-69

Continue burying the waste end of the silk floss up to the butt end of the gut to make a smooth body. Measure and mark the ⅛-inch space for the head and throat. Divide and mark the remaining length of the body into four equal sections. Bring the tying thread back to the first mark.

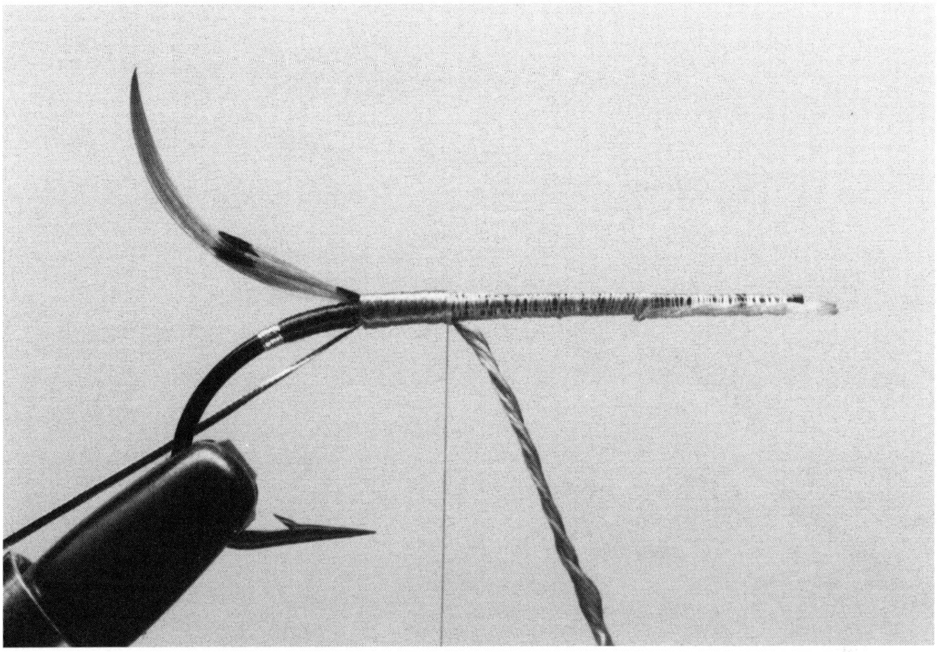

FIGURE 7-70

FIGURE 7-70

Wrap the orange silk floss forward to cover the first section. Tie it off with three turns of thread and cut off the waste end. Complete the fly as shown in figures 7-54 through 7-66, excluding figures 7-60 and 7-61. The Orange Parson has a single pair of golden pheasant tippets, back to back.

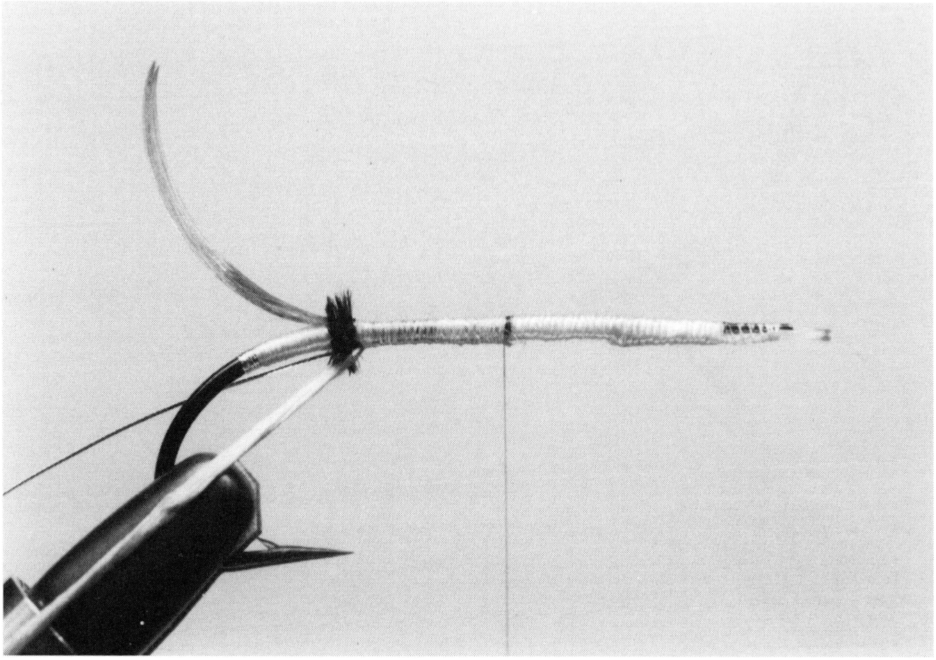

FIGURE 7-71

Jock Scott (plate 9)

Jointed Body with Body Veilings

FIGURE 7-71

Complete the steps in figures 7-1 through 7-12. Note in the photo that the body is not in equal sections and that the posterior is shorter. Tie in the golden yellow silk floss at six o'clock.

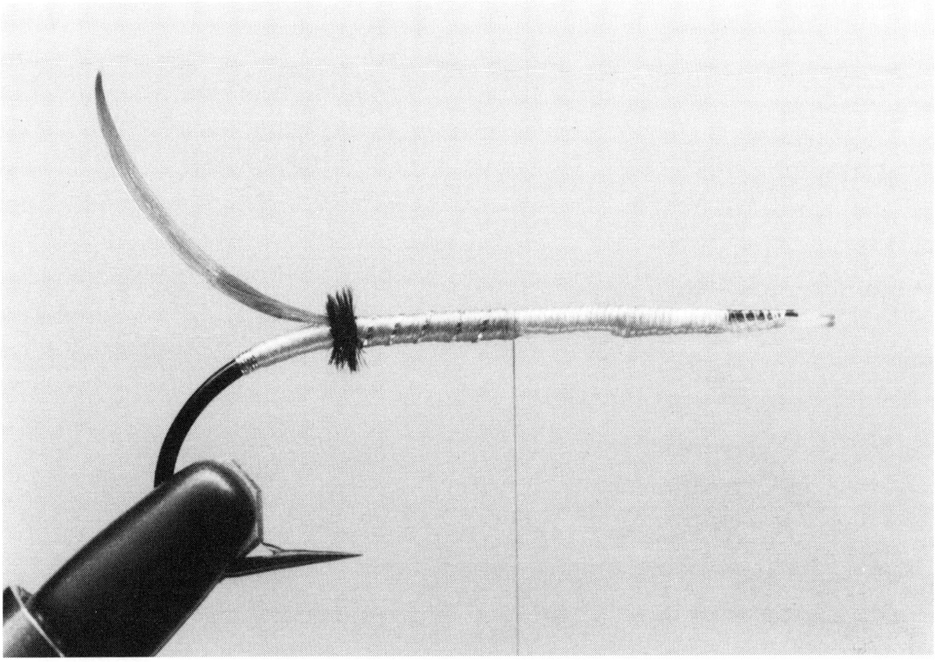

FIGURE 7-72

FIGURE 7-72
Wrap the silk floss forward to the mark. Wrap the fine oval silver tinsel forward, making five turns. Tie off each and cut off the waste ends.

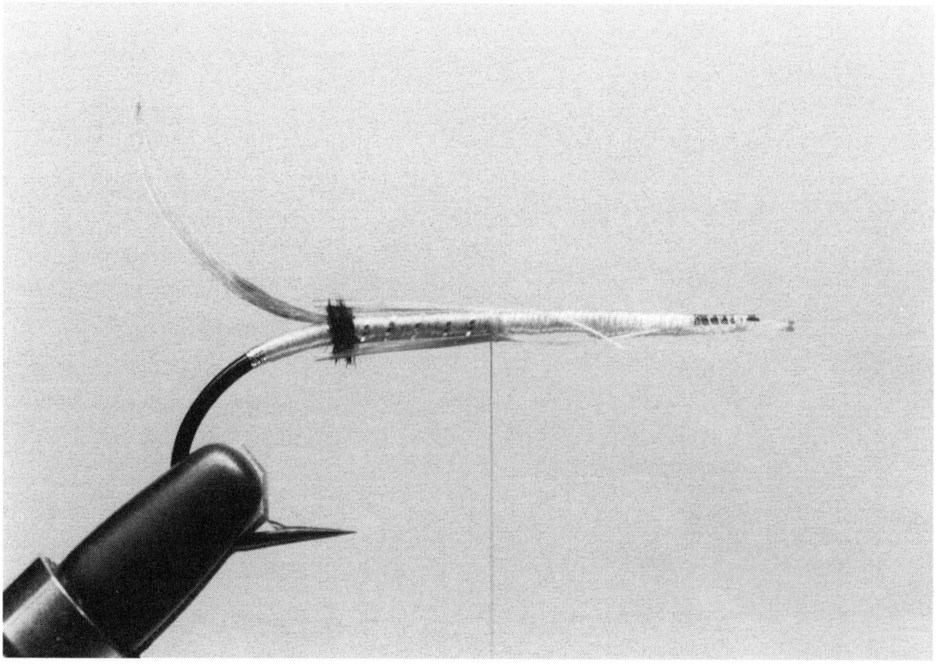

FIGURE 7-73

FIGURE 7-73

Prepare and tie in the toucan body veiling at twelve o'clock and six o'clock. Catch the first couple of barbs with thread so that the quills won't roll.

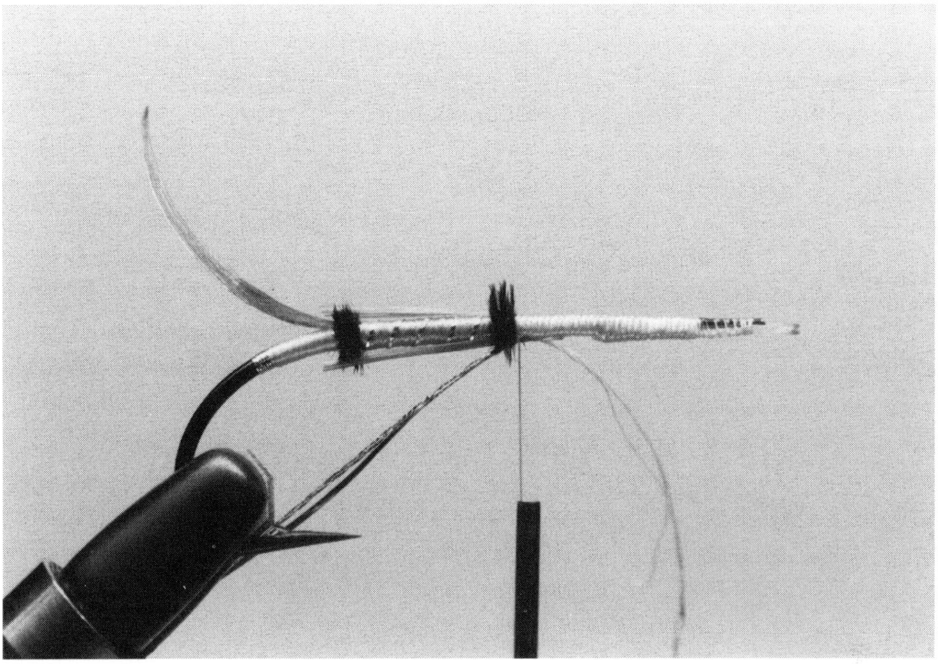

FIGURE 7-74

FIGURE 7-74

Prepare and tie in the middle butt using the same techniques as in figures 7-7 through 7-9. Tie in the silver lace, followed by narrow flat silver tinsel.

FIGURE 7-75

FIGURE 7-75
Double the body hackle and tie it in at six o'clock. Tie in the black silk floss at six o'clock. Use the waste end of the floss to completely smooth out the body. Cut off any remaining waste end of black floss.

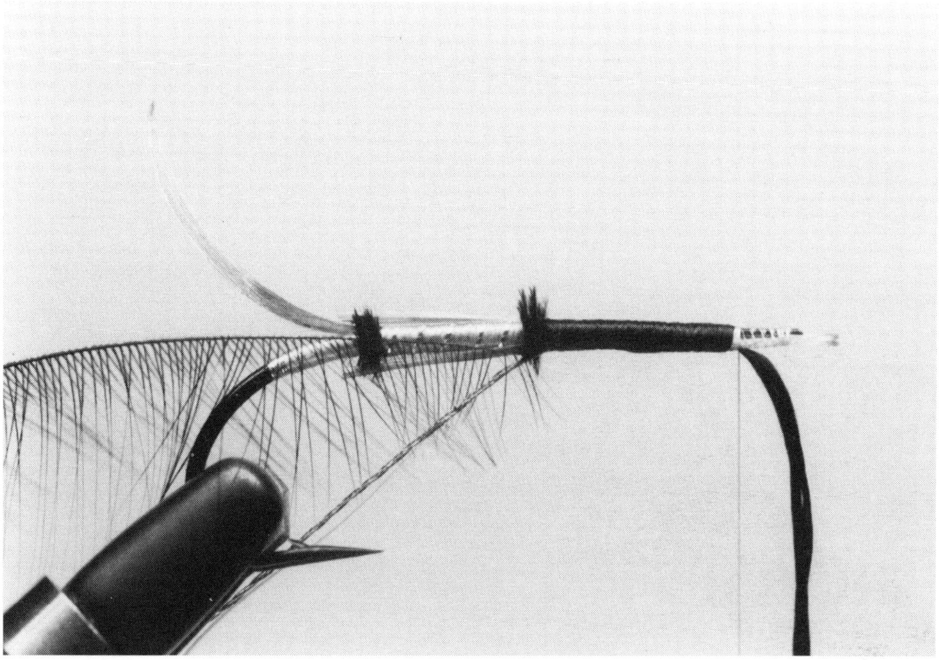

FIGURE 7-76

FIGURE 7-76
Wrap the black silk floss forward to the ⅛-inch mark. Do not cut off the waste end. If there is a slight hump at the end of the gut, it can be flattened by pinching it with a pair of tweezers.

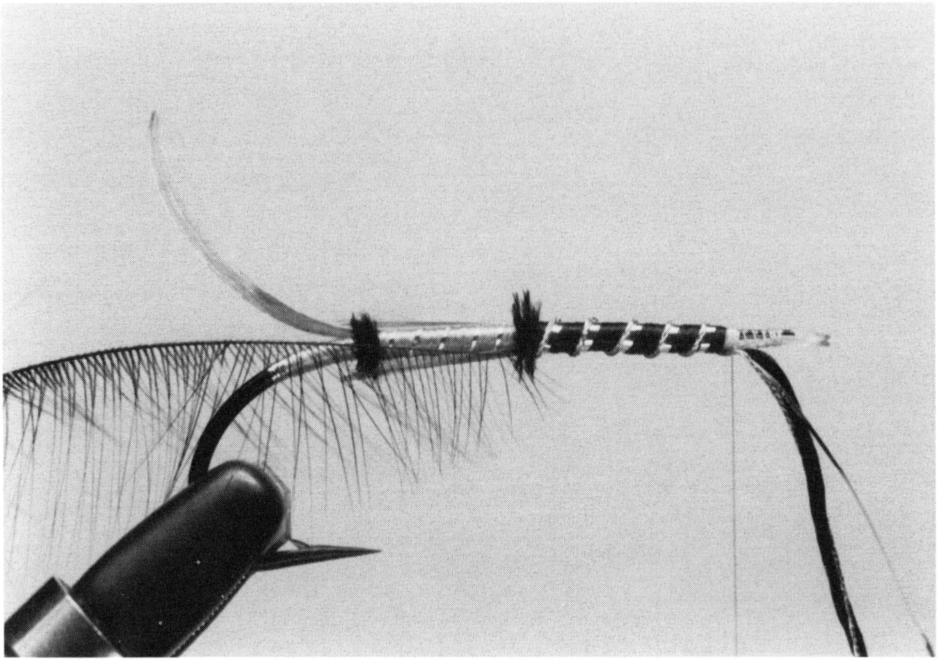

FIGURE 7-77

FIGURE 7-77

Wrap the narrow flat tinsel forward, followed by the silver lace behind it. Tie each but do not cut off the waste ends.

FIGURE 7-78

FIGURE 7-78

Wrap the hackle forward behind the lace. Remove the barbs on top of the hook shank as explained in figure 7-16. Cut off the waste ends of tinsel, silk floss, and hackle. The reason for not cutting waste ends until the anterior section is completed is that if one of the components breaks or pulls out, it is easier to unwrap and tie in the replacement part than to retie that part of the body. This should be a matter of standard practice with the body of any fly.

FIGURE 7-79

FIGURE 7-79

Tie in the throat of speckled guinea fowl as demonstrated in figures 7-17 through 7-20. Tie in the strips of white-tipped turkey following the technique in figure 7-22. Do not cut off the waste ends. Leave them to form a foundation for the wings.

FIGURE 7-80

FIGURE 7-80

Build and tie in the wings by repeating the steps in figures 7-23 through 7-28. The peacock sword barbs are difficult to tie in so that they hug the sides of the wings. The simplest solution is to apply a *very* light coating of liquid wax to the first ⅓ of the butt end of the barb. This will hold them in place until the wing veilings are tied in. Finish the fly using the same techniques as in figures 7-28 through 7-41.

Chapter Eight

A Selection of Dressings

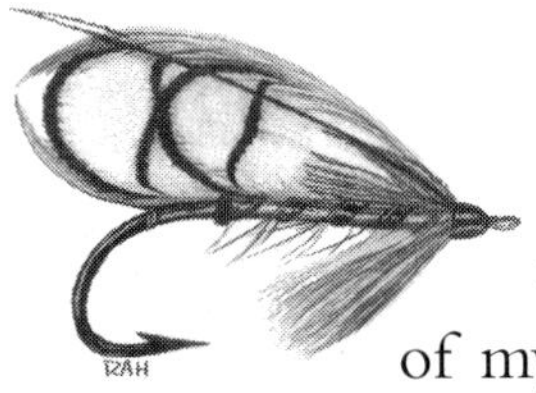

This chapter lists the dressings for twenty-five flies. Most of these are time-honored, but two are of my own design. My reasons for selecting them are twofold: first, their beauty when compared with some of the plainer patterns, and second, their representation of a wide variety of types and styles.

For the sake of custom, I've named the rare feathers in the dressings. For the most part, alternatives can be found in chapter two. The component parts of each fly are tied in in the order in which they are listed. There are some discrepancies between these dressings and those listed in earlier books. This is because some of the earlier dressings emphasized particular parts of the fly that were considered more effective for fishing. These dressings are not always consistent with today's exhibition patterns. An example is a Green Highlander having a tag of only tinsel instead of tinsel and canary floss, which is the way it is listed in the second editions of both Kelson's *The Salmon Fly* and Hale's *How to Tie Salmon Flies*.

Since there are no hard and fast standards in any aspect of building salmon flies, the expression of ability, ingenuity, and individuality is not compromised by a borrowed idea. Everyone who builds featherwing salmon flies has artistic license. Chapter two on alternative materials explains in more detail the reasons for some variations in certain patterns.

Akroyd (Dee Type, Strip Wing)

TAG: Extra-fine oval silver tinsel.

TAIL: Golden pheasant crest.

TAIL VEILING: Golden pheasant tippet in strands.*

RIBS: Medium oval silver tinsel over the orange seal's fur. Fine silver lace and narrow flat tinsel over the black floss.

BODY: First half, light orange seal's fur; second half, black silk floss.

HACKLE: A lemon hackle over the orange seal's fur and a black heron hackle over the black floss.

THROAT: Teal flank.

WINGS: A pair of cinnamon turkey tail strips, set flat. White turkey strips are also used, in which case the pattern is known as the White Winged Akroyd.

CHEEKS: Jungle cock, drooping.

HEAD: Black.

* I use two golden pheasant crests for the tail on all size 4/0 flies.

Baron

TIP: Extra-fine oval silver tinsel.

TAG: Ruby floss.

TAIL: Golden pheasant crest.

TAIL VEILING: Indian crow and blue chatterer (kingfisher).

BUTT: Black ostrich herl.

RIBS: Fine oval silver tinsel in each body section.

BODY: In two equal halves. First half is flat narrow silver tinsel butted with black ostrich herl and veiled above and below with Indian crow; second half is black floss.

HACKLE: Claret over the black floss.

THROAT: European jay.

WINGS: Golden pheasant tippet in strands for the underwing. Married strips of scarlet, blue, and yellow swan; florican; speckled bustard; gray turkey tail; and golden pheasant tail.

WING VEILING: Married strips of teal and barred wood duck. Strips of bronze mallard as a roofing.

CHEEKS: Jungle cock, followed by blue chatterer (kingfisher).

CREST: Golden pheasant crest.

HORNS: Blue-and-yellow macaw.

HEAD: Black.

Beaconfield

TIP: Extra-fine silver twist tinsel.

TAG: Yellow floss.

TAIL: Golden pheasant crest.

TAIL VEILING: Teal and scarlet ibis.

BUTT: Black ostrich herl, followed by two turns of fine oval silver tinsel.

BODY: In three equal sections, the first two doubly butted: that is, number one of yellow silk with a yellow mane* (mohair), black ostrich herl, and two turns of fine silver oval tinsel; number two of red-orange (tippet-color) silk, with a red-orange mane (mohair), black ostrich herl, and two turns of fine silver oval tinsel; number three of claret silk.

THROAT: Light blue hackle.

WINGS: Two golden pheasant tippets (back to back). Married strips of golden pheasant tail; light- and dark-mottled turkey; speckled bustard; yellow, red, and light blue swan. Bronze mallard strips as roofing.

WING VEILING: Strips of teal.

CREST: Golden pheasant crest.

HORNS: Blue-and-yellow macaw.

HEAD: Black.

* A small bunch of mohair tied in at twelve o'clock as a body veiling that extends to or slightly beyond the ostrich herl butt.

Beauly Snow Fly

BODY: Pale blue seal's fur.
RIBS: Broad flat silver tinsel and medium gold lace.
HACKLE: Black heron from the third turn of tinsel.
WINGS: Peacock herl in strands.
HEAD: Orange seal's fur in Pryce-Tannatt; yellow wool in Hale; yellow mohair as a collar tied back in Francis Francis, which looks nice.

Benchill

TAG: Extra-fine oval gold tinsel.

TAIL: Golden pheasant crest.

TAIL VEILING: Tip of a golden pheasant breast feather.

BUTT: Black ostrich herl.

RIBS: Flat narrow silver tinsel and fine silver lace.

BODY: Orange, scarlet, claret, and pale blue seal's fur (well picked out) in equal sections

THROAT: A pale blue hackle.

WINGS: A pair of golden pheasant tippets, back to back; married strips of peacock wing; scarlet and blue swan; golden pheasant tail; and speckled bustard.

WING VEILING: Speckled guinea fowl.

CHEEKS: Jungle cock.

CREST: Golden pheasant crest.

HEAD: Black.

Black Dog

TIP: Extra-fine oval silver tinsel.

TAG: Canary floss.

TAIL: Golden pheasant crest.

TAIL VEILING: Scarlet ibis.

BUTT: Black ostrich herl.

RIBS: Yellow floss with fine oval silver tinsel on each side.

BODY: Black floss.

HACKLE: Black heron from the third turn of tinsel.

WINGS: Two red-orange hackles enveloped by two jungle cock feathers. Married strips of light-speckled bustard; Lady Amherst pheasant tail; and scarlet and yellow swan.

WING VEILING: Unbarred wood duck.

CREST: Two golden pheasant crests.

HEAD: Black.

Butcher

TIP: Extra-fine oval silver tinsel.

TAG: Lemon floss.

TAIL: Golden pheasant crest.

TAIL VEILING: Blue chatterer (kingfisher).

BUTT: Black ostrich herl.

RIBS: Narrow flat silver tinsel and medium silver lace.

BODY: Fiery brown, pale blue, claret, and dark blue seal's fur (well picked out) in equal sections.

HACKLE: Claret or black.

WINGS: A pair of golden pheasant tippets, back to back, covered by a pair of golden pheasant breast feathers, and these by a pair of broad strips of teal. Married strips of yellow swan; speckled bustard; scarlet, blue, and orange swan; and golden pheasant tail. Strips of bronze mallard as roofing.

CHEEKS: Blue chatterer (kingfisher).

CREST: Golden pheasant crest.

HORNS: Blue-and-yellow macaw.

HEAD: Black.

*Canary**

TAG: Extra-fine oval gold tinsel.

TAIL: Golden pheasant tail.

TAIL VEILING: Indian crow.

BODY: Flat silver tinsel in two joints, each joint butted with black ostrich herl and veiled above and below with three or more toucan feathers.

THROAT: Cock-of-the-rock.

WINGS: Six or more golden pheasant crest feathers.

HORNS: Scarlet macaw.

HEAD: Black.

* Pryce-Tannatt's dressing.

Childers

TIP: Extra-fine oval silver tinsel.

TAG: Pale blue floss.

TAIL: Golden pheasant crest.

TAIL VEILING: Indian crow.

BUTT: Black ostrich herl.

RIBS: Medium silver lace and narrow flat silver tinsel.

BODY: Golden yellow floss, orange and fiery brown seal's fur in three equal sections.

HACKLE: A badger dyed yellow.

THROAT: Golden pheasant breast feather followed by widgeon flank.

WINGS: A pair of golden pheasant breast feathers, back to back. Married strips of scarlet, blue, orange, and yellow swan; speckled bustard; florican; golden pheasant tail; cinnamon and mottled-gray turkey tail.

WING VEILING: Strips of wood duck.

CHEEKS: Blue chatterer (kingfisher).

CREST: Golden pheasant crest.

HORNS: Blue-and-yellow macaw.

HEAD: Black.

The Colonel's Lady (Originated by the Author)

TAG: Extra-fine oval gold tinsel.

TAIL: Golden pheasant crest.

TAIL VEILING: Barred wood duck.

BUTT: Black ostrich herl.

RIBS: Fine gold lace and narrow flat gold tinsel.

BODY: Claret floss.

HACKLE: Claret.

THROAT: Kenya crested guinea fowl (alternative, guinea fowl dyed blue).

WINGS: Two pairs of Lady Amherst pheasant tippets, back to back. Tip of the second pair touching the bar of the first pair.

WING VEILING: Jungle cock.

CHEEKS: Kingfisher.

CREST: Golden pheasant crest.

HORNS: Lady Amherst pheasant tail.

HEAD: Black.

Doctor Donaldson

TIP: Extra-fine oval silver tinsel.

TAG: Yellow floss.

TAIL: Golden pheasant crest.

TAIL VEILING: Golden pheasant tippet and toucan.

BUTT: Black ostrich herl.

BODY: First part blue silk floss ribbed with silver oval tinsel, butted with blue chatterer (kingfisher)* and black ostrich herl; second part, claret floss ribbed with silver lace and flat silver tinsel, and claret hackle over.

THROAT: Orange hackle and widgeon.

WINGS: Two extended jungle cock. Married strips of golden pheasant tail; light- and dark-speckled bustard; and red and yellow swan.

CREST: Golden pheasant crest.

WING VEILING: Jungle cock.

HORNS: Blue-and-yellow macaw.

HEAD: Black.

The original pattern called for the jungle cock underwing to be slightly tinged in Bismarck brown color.

* Tied in as a body veiling, followed by a black ostrich herl butt.

Dunkeld

TIP: Extra-fine oval silver tinsel.

TAG: Light orange silk floss.

TAIL: Golden pheasant crest.

TAIL VEILING: A pair of jungle cock, back to back, veiled with a pair of Indian crow feathers, back to back.

BUTT: Black ostrich herl.

BODY: Flat gold tinsel.

RIBS: Fine oval silver tinsel.

HACKLE: Bright orange.

THROAT: European jay.

WINGS: Golden pheasant tippet in strands. Married strips of scarlet, yellow, and blue swan; peacock wing; speckled bustard; florican; golden pheasant tail; and mottled-brown turkey tail. Bronze mallard strips as roofing.

WING VEILING: Jungle cock.

CHEEKS: Blue chatterer (kingfisher).

CREST: Golden pheasant crest.

HORNS: Blue-and-yellow macaw.

HEAD: Black.

Dusty Miller

TIP: Extra-fine oval silver tinsel.
TAG: Golden yellow floss.
TAIL: Golden pheasant crest.
TAIL VEILING: Indian crow.
BUTT: Black ostrich herl.
RIBS: Fine oval silver tinsel.
HACKLE: Golden olive over the orange floss.
BODY: First ⅔ embossed silver tinsel; second ⅓ orange silk floss.
THROAT: Speckled guinea fowl.
WINGS: A pair of white-tipped turkey tail strips, back to back. Married strips of teal; yellow, scarlet, and orange swan; speckled bustard; florican; and golden pheasant tail. Bronze mallard strips as roofing.
WING VEILING: Married strips of pintail and wood duck.
CHEEKS: Jungle cock.
CREST: Golden pheasant crest.
HORNS: Blue-and-yellow macaw.
HEAD: Black.

Evening Star

TIP: Extra-fine oval silver tinsel.

TAG: Tippet-colored (dark orange) floss.

TAIL: Golden pheasant crest.

BUTT: Black ostrich herl.

BODY: In four equal sections: The first three of silver oval tinsel, each having two jungle cock feathers back to back, above and below, butted with black ostrich herl. The last section is blue silk floss and is the only one ribbed with extra-fine oval silver tinsel.

THROAT: Jungle cock. These feathers increase slightly in length from the butt to the throat.

WINGS: Two pairs of Lady Amherst pheasant tippets, back to back. The tip of the second pair should touch the bar of the first pair.

WING VEILING: The tip of a wood duck feather.

CHEEKS: Indian crow.

HORNS: Red macaw tail.

HEAD: Black ostrich herl.

The original pattern calls for a tip of wood duck as the wing veiling. This can mean ⅔ of a whole feather. I prefer a wide strip of wood duck, which does not cover as much of the wing and is more in harmony with the style of other patterns.

Greenwell

TAG: Extra-fine oval silver tinsel.

TAIL: Golden pheasant crest.

TAIL VEILING: A pair of jungle cock, back to back.

BUTT: Black ostrich herl.

RIBS: Broad flat silver tinsel and silver lace.

HACKLE: Pale blue.

BODY: Pale blue floss.

THROAT: Widgeon flank.

WINGS: As in the Dusty Miller, except that the scarlet and orange swan are replaced with blue swan.

CHEEKS: Jungle cock.

CREST: Golden pheasant crest.

HORNS: Blue-and-yellow macaw.

HEAD: Black.

Helmsdale Doctor

TAG: Extra-fine oval silver tinsel.

TAIL: Golden pheasant crest.

TAIL VEILING: Golden pheasant tippets in strands.

BUTT: Scarlet wool.

RIBS: Fine oval silver tinsel.

BODY: Flat silver tinsel.

THROAT: A lemon hackle.

WINGS: Underwing of peacock herl in strands. Married strips of scarlet, blue, orange, yellow, and white swan; cinnamon and light mottled gray turkey tail; and speckled bustard.

CREST: Golden pheasant crest.

HEAD: Scarlet wool.

Highland Gem

TIP: Extra-fine oval silver tinsel.

TAG: Yellow floss.

TAIL: Golden pheasant crest.

TAIL VEILING: Scarlet ibis and barred wood duck.

BUTT: Black ostrich herl.

HACKLE: Black heron on the second body section.

BODY: In two equal sections: First, yellow silk floss ribbed with extra-fine oval silver tinsel and butted with toucan (veiled above and below) and black ostrich herl. Second, blue floss ribbed with extra-fine oval silver tinsel.

THROAT: Speckled guinea fowl.

WINGS: Strips of Lady Amherst pheasant tail and three golden pheasant crests.

HORNS: Black cockatoo (black turkey or goose as an alternative).

HEAD: Black.

Mar Lodge

TAG: Extra-fine oval silver tinsel.

TAIL: Golden pheasant crest.

TAIL VEILING: A pair of jungle cock, back to back.

BUTT: Black ostrich herl.

RIBS: Fine oval silver tinsel.

BODY: Flat silver tinsel, jointed at the middle with three or four turns of black floss.

THROAT: Speckled guinea fowl.

WINGS: Underwing, golden pheasant tippet in strands. Married strips of white swan; speckled bustard; florican; cinnamon, mottled-gray, and mottled-brown turkey tail; and golden pheasant tail.

WING VEILING: Wide strips of wood duck.

CHEEKS: Jungle cock.

CREST: Golden pheasant crest.

HORNS: Blue-and-yellow macaw.

HEAD: Black.

McIntyre

TIP: Extra-fine oval silver tinsel.

TAG: Golden yellow silk floss.

TAIL: Golden pheasant crest.

TAIL VEILING: Indian crow.

BUTT: Black ostrich herl.

RIBS: Medium oval silver tinsel.

HACKLE: Magenta.

BODY: Three turns of orange silk floss, followed by four turns each of red, dark orange, red, and light blue seal's fur.

THROAT: Pale blue hackle and black heron.

WINGS: Two jungle cock, back to back, enveloped by two golden pheasant tippets. Married strips of golden pheasant tail; speckled bustard; peacock wing; and yellow, red, and blue swan. Bronze mallard as roofing.

CREST: Golden pheasant crest.

CHEEKS: Blue chatterer (kingfisher).

HORNS: Red-and-blue macaw.

HEAD: Black wool.

Popham

TAG: Extra-fine oval silver tinsel.

TAIL: Golden pheasant crest.

TAIL VEILING: Indian crow.

BUTT: Black ostrich herl.

RIBS: Extra-fine oval gold tinsel for the first and second sections. Extra-fine oval silver tinsel for the third section.

BODY: In three equal sections of orange, lemon yellow, and pale blue floss. The first and second sections are each butted with black ostrich herl, and all sections are veiled above and below with Indian crow.

THROAT: European jay.

WINGS: Underwing, golden pheasant tippets in strands. Married strips of speckled bustard; florican; peacock wing; scarlet, blue, orange, and yellow swan; and golden pheasant tail. Peacock sword as a wing veiling set high on the sides of the wings.

WING VEILING: Broad strips of wood duck.

CREST: Two or three golden pheasant crests.

HORNS: Blue and yellow macaw.

HEAD: Black.

Red Drummond

TIP: Extra-fine oval silver tinsel.

TAG: Yellow floss.

TAIL: Golden pheasant crest.

TAIL VEILING: Indian crow.

BUTT: Black ostrich herl.

BODY: First half, flat silver tinsel, ribbed with fine oval silver tinsel and veiled above and below with Indian crow. Middle butt of black ostrich herl. Second half, red floss, ribbed with fine oval silver tinsel, and claret hackle over.

THROAT: Speckled guinea fowl.

WINGS: Underwing of white-tipped turkey strips, back to back. Married strips of yellow, red, and blue swan; peacock wing; speckled bustard; golden pheasant tail. Bronze mallard strips as a roofing.

WING VEILING: Married strips of teal and wood duck, followed by jungle cock.

CHEEKS: Blue chatterer (kingfisher).

CREST: Golden pheasant crest.

HORNS: Blue-and-yellow macaw.

HEAD: Black.

Silver Gray

TIP: Extra-fine oval silver tinsel.
TAG: Golden yellow silk floss.
TAIL: Golden pheasant crest.
TAIL VEILING: Wood duck strips, back to back.
BUTT: Black ostrich herl.
RIBS: Fine oval silver tinsel.
HACKLE: A badger hackle.
BODY: Flat silver tinsel.
THROAT: Widgeon flank.
WINGS: Underwing, golden pheasant tippets in strands. Married strips of white, yellow, and green swan; speckled bustard; florican; and golden pheasant tail. Strips of bronze mallard as a roofing.
WING VEILING: Married strips of teal and wood duck.
CHEEKS: Jungle cock.
CREST: Golden pheasant crest.
HORNS: Blue-and-yellow macaw.
HEAD: Black.

Silver Wilkinson

This is the same dressing as the Silver Doctor, except that the throat is magenta, instead of blue, hackle (followed by widgeon). The wool head is omitted, and sometimes Indian crow as well as blue chatterer (kingfisher) is used as a tail veiling. Cheeks of Indian crow and blue chatterer (kingfisher) are added. To quote Pryce-Tannatt, "As is the case with many patterns, however, no two people dress the Silver Wilkinson alike."

Thunder and Lightning

TIP: Extra-fine oval silver tinsel.
TAG: Golden yellow floss.
TAIL: Golden pheasant crest.
TAIL VEILING: Indian crow.
RIBS: Fine oval gold tinsel.
HACKLE: Deep orange.
BODY: Black floss.
THROAT: European jay.
WINGS: Bronze mallard set upright, back to back.
CHEEKS: Jungle cock.
CREST: Golden pheasant crest.
HORNS: Blue-and-yellow macaw.
HEAD: Black.

Yellow Parson

TIP: Extra-fine oval silver tinsel.

TAG: Violet silk floss.

TAIL: Golden pheasant crest.

TAIL VEILING: Golden pheasant tippet.

RIBS: Medium oval silver tinsel.

HACKLE: Yellow.

BODY: Two turns of yellow floss, followed by yellow seal's fur.

THROAT: Scarlet hackle veiled with two golden pheasant crests, side by side.

WINGS: Two golden pheasant tippets, back to back.

WING VEILING: Broad strips of wood duck.

CHEEKS: Blue chatterer (kingfisher).

CREST: Two golden pheasant crests.

HORNS: Blue-and-yellow macaw.

HEAD: Black.

Appendix

Metric Conversion Chart

Listed below are metric equivalents for the traditional English measurements used in this book:

1/32 inch = 0.8 millimeter
1/16 inch = 1.6 millimeters
1/8 inch = 3.2 millimeters
3/16 inch = 4.8 millimeters
1/4 inch = 6.4 millimeters
1/2 inch = 12.7 millimeters
5/8 inch = 15.9 millimeters
15/16 inch = 23.8 millimeters
1 inch = 25.4 millimeters
1 1/16 inches = 27 millimeters
1 1/2 inches = 38.1 millimeters
4 inches = 10.2 centimeters
18 inches = 45.7 centimeters

Bibliography

Bainbridge, George Cole. 1816. *The Fly Fisher's Guide.* London: Longman, Orme, Brown, Green, and Longman.

Blacker, William, 1855. *Blacker's Art of Fly Making.* London: Published by the Author.

Fisher, Maj. A.T. 1892. *Rod and River.* London: Richard Bentley & Son.

Fisher, P. Esq. 1835. *The Angler's Souvenir.* London: Charles Tilt.

Francis, Francis. 1880. *A Book on Angling.* 5th edition. London: Longmans, Green and Co.

Hale, Maj. J.H. 1919. *How to Tie Salmon Flies.* 2d edition. London: The Fishing Gazette, Ltd.

Kelson, George M. 1895. *The Salmon Fly.* London: Published by the Author, c/o Messrs. Wyman & Sons (reprinted 1979, Goshen, Conn.: The Angler's and Shooter's Press; and 1995, Camden, SC: John Culler & Sons).

Maxwell, Sir Herbert. 1898. *Salmon and Sea Trout.* London: George Routledge & Sons, Ltd.; New York: E.P. Dutton & Co.

Pryce-Tannatt, T.E. 1914. *How to Dress Salmon Flies.* London: Adam & Charles Black (reprinted 1986 by the same publisher).

Taverner, Eric. 1935. *Salmon Fishing,* Plymouth, England: The Mayflower Press.

INDEX

Note: Page references in italic indicate color plates, tables, and sidebars. Boldface references indicate illustrations and photographs.